"But one thing I do: Forgetting what is behind and straining toward what is ahead, I press on toward the goal to win the prize for which God has called me heavenward in Christ Jesus."

—Philippians 3:13–14 (NIV)

WHISTLE STOP
Café
MYSTERIES

LET IT SNOW

BECKY MELBY

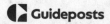

Whistle Stop Café Mysteries is a trademark of Guideposts.

Published by Guideposts
100 Reserve Road, Suite E200
Danbury, CT 06810
Guideposts.org

Cover and interior design by Müllerhaus
Cover illustration by Greg Copeland at Illustration Online LLC.
Typeset by Aptara, Inc.

ISBN 978-1-961125-93-3 (hardcover)
ISBN 978-1-961125-94-0 (epub)

Printed and bound in the United States of America
10 9 8 7 6 5 4 3 2 1

LET IT SNOW

December 1, 1942

Margie McGarry hurried across the wood floor of the Dennison, Ohio, train depot, straining under the weight of the large box she carried. The overflowing mound of fresh-from-the-fryer cake doughnuts threatened to collapse the box...or her. Her stomach growled as deep-fried sweetness wafted up from the golden-brown circles of temptation. Once again, she'd overslept and chosen time in front of the mirror instead of breakfast with her parents. When she rose only half an hour before the arrival of a troop train, perfect Betty Grable rolls in her shoulder-length auburn hair and a well-drawn hunter's bow on her top lip were much higher priorities than Mom's latest egg creation.

"Eggs," Margie said to herself with an exasperated sigh. She'd been thrilled when her father purchased a dozen fuzzy baby chicks right before Easter. She'd joined her parents and brother in celebrating the first egg in July, and they'd all studied how to keep the hens

WHISTLE STOP CAFÉ MYSTERIES

laying into the winter. Four months into their eggstrav-aganza, the joy was waning. "Scotch eggs. Spinach soufflé. Egg casserole. Scrambled, fried, over-easy, over-hard, poached, boiled, sunny-side up," she mumbled under her breath. If she were still at Kent State where she should be, she'd have meat at least once a day. But she was where she belonged. Her brother had enlisted two months ago, and she was needed here, working at her family's furniture factory, serving doughnuts to soldiers with the Salvation Army and eating what her father called "Mother's eggsperiments."

But there was just so much a person could take. One of the depot volunteers had suggested they make ornaments out of eggs...after blowing out the contents. Which meant she'd have to put her lips on a raw egg and watch the goo slither out. Her stomach lurched at the thought. With another sigh, this one wistful, she whispered, "If I never see another egg after this war is over, it will be too soon."

"Too soon for what?"

Margie startled, and a doughnut rolled off the top of the pile right into the hands of gum-snapping Esther Davis. Though a hoot to work with, Esther had a one-track mind that often earned her "the look" from Molly O'Sullivan, the woman in charge of depot volunteers.

"Here they come!" As the low rumble of an approaching train grew louder, Esther grabbed a waxed-paper-wrapped popcorn ball from a table and pretended to pitch it toward the window. In honor of the holiday season, they'd used beet juice to color them red. Well reddish. And nothing they tried created a Christmassy green. "Did you put your name and address in any?" Esther asked. She had written her contact information on tiny pieces of paper and hidden them under the waxed paper on several of them that she set aside, in case she met a soldier she wanted to get to know better.

Margie shook her head and set the box of dough-nuts down next to a pyramid of sandwiches made by Molly Sullivan's next-door neighbor's girls. The oldest, Madeline, held a ham and cheese in each hand. The concentration on her face rivaled that of a pitcher winding up on the mound. Margie skirted around the end of the long table, ready to serve doughnuts hand over fist for the next fifteen minutes. "I don't want a wartime romance," she said. "Way too hard."

"I prefer to think of them as challenging." Esther smoothed shimmery blond waves. "The biggest chal-lenge being keeping them all straight. Ooh. Now there's a couple of dreamboats for you." She batted her eyelashes as the first few soldiers strode through the door. Suddenly, one stepped aside, jostling the man next to him, as another soldier darted around them and took off, almost at a run.

Margie froze. The man was silhouetted by the bright sunlight behind him. But even though she couldn't make out his features, she'd know that frame, that posture. That gait. He strode away from the halo of light, and his face came into sharp focus. She knew that face. Every angle, crease, and smile line.

"Jesse!" she shouted.

But the swell of voices and shuffle of feet drowned out his name.

CHAPTER ONE

Balancing two boxes of Christmas decorations in her arms, Debbie Albright walked down the front steps of the craftsman-style house she'd lived in for the last six months, and then she turned back to admire her handiwork. After an already restless night filled with too many memories, she'd been startled awake by sirens and crawled out of bed long before the first-day-of-December sun's rays had seeped through the curtains.

While sipping a cup of reheated gingerbread-spiced mocha latte and listening to Christmas carols earlier, she'd decked a grapevine wreath with sprigs of holly, pinecones, and a smattering of bright red berries, finishing it off with a big, cheery buffalo plaid bow. Now, as she studied the wreath from the sidewalk, she smiled a bit brighter and cheerier than she actually felt and then straightened her shoulders and lifted her chin. This *would* be a good Christmas. And by the time she finished decorating, here and at work, all doubts about calling Dennison home again would vanish.

Wouldn't they?

With a wistful sigh, she continued her short walk to work, breathing in the crisp morning air as she reflected on past holiday seasons here in her hometown. Dennison, Ohio, did Christmas well. And now she was part of making that happen.

As she approached the train depot that housed the Whistle Stop Café, which she owned and operated with her longtime best friend, Janet Shaw, she scrolled through her mental checklist of the day's chores. "Change the Flavor of the Day on the chalkboard from gingerbread spice to roasted chestnut, put up the tree, order more—"

Her words faltered on a whoosh of breath that crystallized in midair. Something was missing. Beneath the arched trusses supporting the depot roof, a large empty space gaped like a toothless smile. The brick surrounding the space had faded with time, making the empty spot more pronounced.

The wooden bench, scarred with names and dates carved over eight decades, was gone. "How? Who would—"

"Where's the bench?" Janet's stunned voice joined hers. Debbie hadn't even heard her come out of the café.

"I have no idea. It was here when we left yesterday. Wasn't it?"

"Yes, I'm sure it was." Janet's brow creased over her hazel eyes dimming with confusion. She shook her head. "We would have noticed if it was gone. *Someone* would have."

"Maybe the village had it sent out to be refinished or repaired or something. Kim will know." Kim Smith, curator of the depot museum, was also on the village board.

"Terrible timing if they did."

"I know." The idea of the bench being "sent out" for anything had sounded lame when she suggested it. The old oak bench had to weigh well over a hundred pounds, and it had been bolted to the concrete. Any needed maintenance could be done much more easily right where it was. And, as Janet had just pointed out, the timing would be awful.

"Who does it actually belong to anyway?"

"Um…" Debbie stared at her friend. "I'm not sure. It would have been the property of the Pennsylvania Railroad at one time. But the village owns the depot, so I imagine 'we the people' own the bench."

The sound of car tires crunching gravel made them turn in tandem. Kim got out. "Morning! What are you two— Where's the bench?"

"You don't know?" Debbie felt the stir of uneasiness she'd awakened with returning.

"No clue."

Kim took her keys out of her purse, and the jingle broke the quiet. "Let's get ready for the day and start making phone calls. I'll call the president of the village board. If he doesn't know, I'll call the mayor. It's not like someone would just up and steal it in the middle of the night. Right?" She turned to Janet and Debbie for confirmation, but all she got in return was a weak smile from Janet and a shrug from Debbie.

A dim light bulb flickered in the back of Debbie's mind. A memory from many years earlier. "I'll call my mother. She wrote to me once about a couple of women who were in a heated debate about the bench. One thought it was an eyesore, the other said it was an icon of Dennison history." Debbie had lived an hour and a half north, in Cleveland, from the time she'd started college until she'd moved back in June. Every week for twenty-five years her mother had sent a newsy letter, first by snail mail and then email, chock-full of town gossip. "Either of you remember that?"

Kim and Janet both shook their heads. "I've been working here for twenty years," Kim said, "and I don't remember hearing about it."

"It's a long shot. The women might already be gone, but it's a place to start."

Kim opened the door, and they entered, all three stopping to scan the inside of the depot as if sharing the same thought. Was anything else missing?

Debbie's gaze swept from the marred plank floor to the vaulted ceiling of the depot's waiting area, refurbished to replicate the way it would have appeared during the heyday of the railroad. She looked at the familiar artifacts from days gone by. The original depot clock, its face yellowed but still keeping perfect time. Several rusty lanterns, some with yellow glass, some with red, the kind that would have been swung to tell trains to slow or stop.

Pulling out her own keys, Debbie opened the door to the café. She scanned the space that had seemed to call her name back in the spring when the idea of reopening the old café first came to her. From the wood flooring to bright yellow walls and white pressed-tin ceiling. She stepped over to the antique cash register, set the boxes down, and stared up at the black-and-white photograph of a group of women standing behind a rolling cart filled with small paper bags. In front of them was a sign that read THE SALVATION ARMY CANTEEN. FREE SERVICE TO SERVICEMEN AND SERVICEWOMEN.

Everything appeared to be in order. Nothing to do now but start the day. And pray. *Lord, help us figure this out. Soon.*

"We need that bench," Janet said, echoing the thoughts in Debbie's head.

"I know." Debbie sighed as she reached for a pink candy-cane-print apron. "We spent more money than we should have on those postcards." She walked to the counter and picked up a glossy card displaying a photograph of a smiling couple sitting on the iconic—and now missing—bench. Two small children in footy pajamas snuggled on their laps, apple cheeks rosy as they smiled. The caption read, *Come have your picture taken in front of the Dennison Depot, enjoy a fresh-from-the-oven treat at the Whistle Stop Café, then ride the Dennison Christmas Train!*

Janet tapped her finger on the card. "I don't think it's a coincidence that these cards went out three days ago."

Debbie's shoulders fell. This was not the way to start the season she was determined to make merry and bright. "I don't want to agree with you, and we won't know until we've made those calls, but I think you're right." She glanced out the front window. "It's no coincidence."

"I can't remember. That was over twenty years ago." Becca Albright, Debbie's mother, leaned her elbows on the café counter as she sipped a cup of roasted chestnut coffee sweetened with a dollop of maple syrup. On her way to her part-time receptionist job, she wore a black cardigan over a crisp white blouse and black pants. A glittery green Christmas tree pin softened the severity of her professional attire. She squinted at her daughter. "You look tired, sweetie."

"I woke up before dawn," Debbie said. She turned to Janet. "Did you hear the sirens?"

"Ian was called out early. All I know is there was an accident out on Stillwater." Janet's husband, Ian, was Dennison's chief of police.

"Oh!"

Debbie raised an eyebrow at her mother's sudden exclamation. "It was Rita Carson and Doris Kimball." She shrugged. "Your dad always teases me about the way my brain connects dots. 'Stillwater' reminded me of the summer I spent in Stillwater, Minnesota, with my grandparents when I was little and met my cousins who lived in Kimball, Minnesota. And that made me think of Doris Kimball. Anyway, those two almost split the town in half over the depot bench back in…must have been 1999. I've never since seen such a fierce debate at a town meeting. You remember Doris, right?"

Debbie nodded as she unpacked a box of bright red mugs she'd ordered just for the season. "Of course." Doris Kimball had played a major role in fostering Debbie's love of reading. "She was the stereotypical librarian. And Sunday school teacher. Very kind but very serious. She still is. And even in retirement she doesn't talk over a whisper. I can't picture her involved in a heated debate."

"She sure came out of her shell during that meeting. The council president had to use his gavel a couple of times just to break up the argument. I guess her passion overcame her shyness."

"I have much more vivid memories of Mrs. Carson." Debbie still felt a twinge of fear when she thought of the stern-faced fifth-grade teacher. "They called her 'the warden.' Do you remember how terrified I was before I found out I'd be in Mrs. Stebinski's room?"

Her mother laughed. "You threatened to run away, as I recall."

"No one wanted to be in her class. She was mean. I can definitely imagine her raising a ruckus about the bench. But why? Why did it matter so much to her?"

"I know. I always wondered that myself. I think there was something going on that none of us knew about."

"Hmm." Debbie rinsed a red cup then dried it and hung it on a wrought iron mug tree she'd found in the storeroom. "I think—" She stopped when Kim hurried into the café, the look on her face saying she couldn't wait to share something.

"Morning, Becca. Sorry to interrupt. I talked to three village board members. The board didn't order moving the bench. I also talked to the mayor. She has a theory. *Ohio Heritage* magazine is announcing an online contest to discover which Ohio Christmas town is the most beloved by their readers. They're sending out reporters and photographers to take pictures of 'nostalgic Christmas scenes' in the five towns they've nominated, and then they'll ask their followers to vote on the one that best depicts 'The Heart of Ohio at Christmas.' Dennison is one of the five!"

"Seriously?" Debbie looked at Janet, who was adding apple fritters to the display case but clearly listening.

Janet hurried over. "Dennison made the list? That's huge. *Ohio Heritage* has thousands of subscribers. For Dennison to make the top five is great advertising, whether we win or not."

Kim nodded. "Their reporter and photographer are coming here on December sixteenth. They want pictures of the depot and train, and they specifically mentioned the bench. We have to find it before then."

Debbie frowned. "So…you said the mayor had a theory. Is she thinking one of the other towns is trying to sabotage our chances of winning?"

"That's exactly what she's thinking."

"So who else is on the list?" Janet asked.

"Cambridge, Coshocton, Lebanon, and Clifton."

"We need to go talk to the editors." Debbie stepped behind the counter and picked up the latest print edition of the magazine. Every month, she and Janet took turns paging through *Ohio Heritage* when the café wasn't busy. "Where is this published?" She opened the front cover and perused the tiny print on the first page until she found the address. "Coshocton."

"That's only forty-five minutes away," Kim said.

"Home of the Roscoe Barbeque Company," Janet said. "I'm thinking we might need to take a drive after we close this afternoon." Her eyes twinkled. It was no secret that Janet loved good barbecue.

Debbie grinned. "I'm in." The restaurant, located in Historic Roscoe Village, had the best smoked brisket she'd ever tasted. The Village, a recreated nineteenth-century canal town, offered self-guided living history tours, inviting visitors to interact with the town's doctor, printer, weaver, blacksmith, and broom maker. Taking a short road trip might be just what she needed to get out of her head for a bit. "Think we can put in a good word for Dennison while we're there?"

"We can try," Kim said. "And if we give them a picture of the bench, maybe we can convince them to send it to their photographers across the state and ask them to keep an eye out for it. Though I can't believe anyone would be so brazen as to have it out where it can be seen. I'm thinking it's probably well hidden somewhere."

The bell above the café door jingled, and Harry Franklin, one of Dennison's oldest residents, ambled in, leaning on the arm of his granddaughter, Patricia. Crosby, Harry's pet and the café's unofficial four-legged mascot, trotted in behind them.

"Where is my bench?" Harry's uncharacteristically gruff voice carried across the café. Harry had been a porter at the depot during World War II and then a train conductor for years after that. He was retired now, and much of his day was spent sitting on the depot bench. If anyone had a right to call it his, Debbie supposed it would be him.

The black-and-white dog who lived with Harry and followed him everywhere looked up with a dejected expression in his big brown eyes, as if to echo Harry's question. Crosby spent as much time at that bench as his owner did.

"We don't know what happened to it, but we're hoping to find out." Debbie motioned to Harry's favorite table, right in front of the window. "Maybe you can help us solve the mystery." She stepped past him and pulled out the chair facing the tracks.

Patricia took the chair across from her grandfather. "We'll each have a cinnamon roll. Hold the calories in mine."

Debbie smiled. "Two fresh-from-the-oven cinnamon rolls, one sans calories, coming right up." She turned on her heel. She didn't need to ask what they wanted to drink. Unadulterated black coffee for Harry. He often said, "Like it was back in the day when the pot sat on the woodstove from morning to night. Loved that last cup of the day." Peppermint mocha for his granddaughter.

As Debbie filled their mugs behind the counter, she whispered to Janet, "Think I'll go join them for a bit."

"Good idea." Janet opened a drawer and took out a pen and the notebook they used for a running list of things they needed to order. "Take notes. I'll heat up their cinnamon rolls."

Debbie tucked pen and notebook into her apron pocket and carried two red mugs to the table. "Mind if I join you?" she asked.

"Not at all," Harry said, pointing to the chair next to Patricia.

Debbie sat and then pulled out the notebook. "We have no idea who took the bench. You know everyone in town, Harry. We need a list of suspects. Who do—"

"You aren't going to need that. We don't need a list. Only one name to write down. There's only one person I know foolish enough and strong enough to take my bench."

CHAPTER TWO

There's only one person I know foolish enough and strong enough to take my bench. Debbie waited while Harry scowled into his coffee. She had no idea who he was talking about. She glanced at Patricia. The creases between her chocolate-brown eyes said she wasn't pleased with the way this conversation was going. Patricia rested a hand on Harry's arm. "You know that's not true, Pop Pop."

Debbie waited while Harry continued to aim his anger at the brew in his red cup. Finally, she broke the silence with one word. "Who?"

"Michael Morgan." Harry growled the name through gritted teeth.

Debbie knew who he was only because he was on the village board. She thought he might somehow be connected to the family-owned McGarry-Morgan Furniture Company. "So, if he had it removed, it would have been approved by the whole board, right?" But Kim said the board hadn't approved it.

"Not necessarily. The man who broke my granddaughter's heart because her family wasn't good enough for his does not play by the rules."

Michael Morgan was Patricia's ex? Patricia had gone by her maiden name for so long, Debbie would have been hard-pressed to remember her married name. It had been years since her divorce. Why would the man be seeking revenge now?

"Pop Pop." Patricia looked absolutely mortified. Though in her professional life as an attorney she certainly faced formidable opponents, she seemed incapable of standing up to this man she adored. She sighed and said to Debbie, "My ex can be…I guess *retaliatory* would be the right word."

"Retaliatory?" Harry's left hand closed in a fist. "He totaled her car, on purpose, after she told him she was leaving. Leaving because he was a no-good, dishonest, cheating—"

"That's enough, Pop Pop. We have no reason to believe Michael had anything to do with this."

"I have reason!" Harry thumped his fist on the table. Debbie had never seen this side of him. "That last Christmas you were together, after you were pretending to be all happy when we had our picture taken on my bench, Michael up and kicked it and said it was a piece of junk and needed to be replaced."

Janet silently set two plates on the table, made eye contact with Debbie, and then stepped back and pressed her hands together, indicating she was praying.

Debbie hoped the sweet, cinnamon-laden aroma of the warm rolls would soften Harry's mood, but he didn't even glance at them. She was almost afraid to insert herself into the conversation, but something needed to diffuse Harry's anger and get him focused on facts. "Michael is connected to the furniture factory?"

Patricia nodded. "He's the vice president. But I don't think—"

"He's big as an ox. He could have hefted my bench onto his shoulder and walked off like he was carrying a sack of potatoes."

Patricia slid her hand over her face, and the bell over the door jangled. Debbie looked up to see Ian walk in. Janet scurried toward him and hugged him. Debbie tried to ignore a twinge of envy. Janet's police chief husband was tall, handsome, and strong, the kind of man every young girl dreamed of marrying. Her best friend had a knight in shining armor, and even though Debbie was thrilled for her, sometimes the comparison to her own solitary life was just plain hard. She fought the swell of emotions, and Janet curled her index finger, motioning for Debbie to join them. She stood and turned to face Patricia. "How would you feel about us trying to talk to Michael?"

"Don't go alone," Harry said.

Patricia shook her head. "He's not that… He's not dangerous."

But Debbie didn't miss the pain in her voice that hinted of bad memories that hadn't yet faded.

Ian slid onto a stool at the counter, and Janet brought him a cup of roasted chestnut coffee. When Debbie walked over, Janet turned to her with a look of concern. And a hint of fear. "Ashling Kelly was in that accident. She's in surgery right now."

"Oh no." Debbie mirrored Janet's expression, but she knew this had to be hitting Janet and Ian much harder. The girl with the unique Irish name who'd graduated from high school in the spring was one of their daughter Tiffany's closest friends.

Janet held out her hands, and Debbie and Ian each took one.

As she prayed along with Janet for Ashling and anyone else involved in the accident, Debbie pictured bright green eyes and Ashling's long auburn braid. After doing odd jobs the last few summers, she had started her own "Jill of All Trades" business, offering to do anything from grocery shopping to painting, home repair, and helping people move. She was a frequent customer, always ordering a cake doughnut with chocolate frosting and coffee with "lots of room for cream and sugar."

Ian filled them in on the details he knew so far. "Her truck was totaled. When I saw that brand-new red Silverado wrapped around…" He shook his head, and Debbie was glad he hadn't finished the sentence. "Looks like a single-car accident, but my guys are still combing the scene just to be sure."

"So sad," Debbie whispered. Ashling lived with her grandmother, Colleen Kelly. Debbie wasn't sure of the reasons. She knew that Ashling's mom, young and single when she found she was expecting, had tried to raise her for a few years then left her with Colleen. She wondered if someone was with Colleen in the waiting room at the hospital.

Janet rested her fingertips on Ian's arm. "Tell Debbie what you heard across the street."

"I pulled up in front of the depot, and just as I noticed the bench was gone, one of the Realtors ran out of their office and called me over. She said they saw a 1950s mint-green pickup drive by here a number of times yesterday afternoon. It slowed down every time it passed the depot."

"Sounds suspicious." Debbie turned to the window. "Did they get a license plate number?"

"No. She apologized all over for that. It would have helped to be able to look it up, but I'm pretty sure if I put out a BOLO—Be On The Lookout—for a 1950s mint-green pickup, my guys will find it if it's in the area."

Janet nodded. "It's a lead anyway."

"A lead?" Ian laughed. "So you've already determined a crime has been committed?"

Janet frowned at him. "Don't laugh. We've been right on things like this before. And we've checked out all the simpler explanations."

Ian held up both hands in surrender. "Who am I to argue with women's intuition? You two have been right more times than I can count." He glanced toward the café entrance. "Have you checked footage from the security cameras?"

Janet shook her head. "I thought of that, but they're all pointed at the entrances. None of them are aimed at the bench."

Debbie set her notebook on the counter and wrote *Harry thinks Patricia's ex, Michael Morgan, might have taken the bench* then turned the notebook around and slid it to Ian.

Ian nodded. "He has priors. Guess it wouldn't surprise me too much. Revenge is a pretty powerful motive. I'll take a minute to chat with Harry and Patricia."

"Good," Debbie said.

Ian stood and picked up his cup. Debbie watched him walk over to Harry and Patricia's table and then motioned for Janet to follow her to the far end of the counter.

As they stood together, Debbie filled Janet in on what she'd learned about Michael Morgan. "Do you know him? Or anyone from his family?"

Janet gave a slow nod. "Not really. But I remember Patricia saying once that he had a hair-trigger temper."

"And, like Ian said, revenge is a powerful motive." Debbie pulled the drip tray out of the cappuccino machine and walked to the sink.

As she did, she glanced at the promo postcard on the counter. The photo had been taken on a warm day in October. They'd decorated the bench with garland and big red bows and dumped bags of biodegradable artificial snow around it. The picture-perfect family sat on the bench, smiling like they weren't overheating in knit hats and puffy jackets. It had been a fun day. Debbie smiled at the memory then froze as a detail she'd seen hundreds of times suddenly jumped out at her.

"Janet. Do you see that?" She pointed at a heart carved into the back of the bench, exactly in the center, right between the parents' shoulders. Though the bottom was hidden by one arm of a pink jacket, enough was visible to read *JB & MM*.

Janet bent down for a closer look then turned to Debbie with confusion etched on her face.

"'MM.' It could stand for Michael Morgan."

"Hmm. I suppose it could. I know it was there when Ian carved our initials." Janet's face glowed, and she grinned.

For the second time in the space of minutes, Debbie pushed down feelings she could only give vent to after work. She nodded but didn't say the words whispering in her mind. She didn't say, "They were there when Reed carved ours too." So many years had passed since the day she still thought of as one of the happiest of her life. The day Reed Brandt, without her knowing, asked her father's permission to marry her then later knelt before her and proposed.

She'd been engaged for a year when her fiancé, the only man she'd ever loved, was killed in Afghanistan. In December. They'd planned a Christmas wedding for the following year. The number of years that had passed didn't matter. This was still always a difficult season. Would she ever be able to celebrate Christmas without this melancholy haze hanging over her head? She rinsed the drip tray, shook off the excess water, and shook away the thoughts at the same time.

"But there's one problem with that," Janet said. "It says 'MM & JB' not 'MM & PF.'"

Debbie gave a decisive nod. "Exactly. What if 'JB' is why Michael and Patricia aren't still together?"

"So he stole the whole bench to...what? Cover up his infidelity with an old girlfriend?"

"Or...something."

Janet's gaze arched up but stopped short of an eye roll. Debbie could tell she wasn't buying any of this theory. To be honest, it did seem far-fetched. But so did the idea that Michael Morgan walked away with the depot bench balanced on his shoulder because he wanted to get even with Harry.

Ian stood, waved to Harry, and walked back to the end of the counter where Janet was opening a box of honey packets. Debbie stepped closer, and Ian said, "All I learned is that they've never seen Michael Morgan in a green pickup and he prefers new cars. And that Harry blames himself for thinking Michael was a great catch for his granddaughter and encouraging their relationship."

A sharp but muffled bark came from Crosby and was answered by a louder bark Debbie instantly recognized. Hammer was the black-and-white border collie that accompanied the president of Dennison's Chamber of Commerce wherever he went. Janet nudged her. "I believe this is your customer, ma'am." Her eyes glinted.

Debbie felt a sudden rush of jitters. Ridiculous at her age. But she was so out of practice at this mutual attraction thing. That was all she'd let herself call it. Greg Connor was an amazing man. Godly, caring, funny, with a passion for history that matched her own. Besides being brilliant at creating networking opportunities for the town's businesses, he also flipped houses and was single-handedly raising two boys. And therein lay the problem that caused the jitters. Julian was a seventh grader, and Jaxon had started high school this year. Great kids. She had a good rapport with Julian, but she couldn't let this relationship, whatever it was, get much deeper until she found a way to break through the barrier that kept Jaxon at a distance. Greg had trained his boys well, and Jaxon was always polite, but behind the right words, his disapproval came across loud and clear. She knew it probably had nothing to do with her in particular, but her presence upset the balance. It was her daily prayer that she'd find a way to bridge the distance between herself and Greg's older son.

The bell above the door jingled, and Debbie's heart switched to double time. Greg's brown canvas jacket was unzipped, revealing a cobalt-blue shirt that perfectly matched his eyes. Eyes so blue she sometimes felt she was floating in the middle of an expansive summer sky when she looked into them.

Stop that! This schoolgirl crush, complete with silly metaphors, was getting out of hand. She smiled at Greg and told him she'd bring his coffee. Just the way he liked it. Cream and one packet of raw sugar. "Cinnamon roll or doughnut?"

"Cinnamon roll, please." He stepped toward the counter. "What happened to that bench out front?"

Janet pointed to the table behind Harry and Patricia's. "Instead of sitting at the counter, why don't you go sit in a comfier seat, and Debbie will come tell you all about it." With a gentle but insistent push in the middle of Debbie's back, she whispered, "I'll bring the coffee and rolls. For both of you."

"But—"

"No buts. I know December can be hard for you. I get that. But it's time to start looking at the future that's right in front of you, friend. A big, bright, handsome, blue-eyed future. Now go."

December 1, 1942

Uniformed men swarmed into the depot, forming a line in front of Esther and Helen Brown, who had been dubbed "Sandwich Sweetie" by an army lieutenant. In seconds, the first man in line reached Margie, and she could only steal furtive glances at her best friend's brother, the man she'd had one single date with before he enlisted. The man she prayed for every night.

Amid a steady stream of "Hey, cookie," "Thanks, doll," and "Aren't you a sight for sore eyes," she tried to track Jesse's movements in her peripheral vision.

He was second in line for the telephone. A line thirty deep formed behind him. He looked at his watch and shifted his weight from one foot to the other. What she could see of his face was tight and drawn. When the man in front of him stepped away, Jesse gripped the receiver in one hand. The other was balled in a tight fist. So not like Jesse. She'd often teased him about lacking a pulse. He was always calm, no matter the crisis or drama whirling around him. There had been both in the year they were at Kent State University. A girl in Margie's dorm had threatened suicide when her boyfriend dumped her, but Jesse had calmed her with that soft, warm voice of his. She'd never seen him this agitated. What was the cause of all that tension?

Margie's box of doughnuts was three-fourths gone when she saw Jesse slam down the receiver, kick the wall, and turn around. He pulled a notebook from his pocket, ripped out a page, and pressed it against the wall as he wrote something. Then his eyes zeroed in on her.

"Cover for me, Esther?" Margie asked.

"You got it, honey. But that guy looks like heart trouble for a girl who says she doesn't want any."

Margie dashed from behind the table. When she was within a yard of Jesse, she stopped but couldn't withhold the grin spreading across her face.

"I was praying you'd be here." His voice was tight and breathless.

The words washed over her. She reached up to hug him. But he grabbed her forearms then let go of one and tugged her into the shadows behind the open office door. His grip hurt a little. "Jesse. What in the—"

"I don't have time to explain." He stuffed a wadded paper into her palm and closed her fingers around it. "I need you to send this in a telegram to Andrea. Exactly as it is. Don't mention my name or yours. She'll know who sent it."

"What's it about?"

Jesse glanced over her head then drilled into her with that steady gaze she'd come to adore. Only this time it reminded her of roiling storm clouds. "It's a matter of national security."

She gave a soft gasp, and his hands tightened around hers. "I'm sorry for putting you in this position, Margie. I'll make it up to you. I promise." The train whistle blew, and he pulled her into his arms. "I promise," he whispered into her hair.

And then he was gone.

The depot emptied, leaving a haunting quiet. Margie looked down, slowly opened the paper, and read words that made no sense.

Tell Father not to give the gold ring from David King's friend for Christmas Eve. The man can't be trusted.

CHAPTER THREE

On Friday afternoon, Debbie changed into stretch jeans and a heather-gray sweater with a line of pearls along each sleeve. With the addition of short black boots that fit like gloves, she was ready for the drive to Coshocton. As she slid her arms into a suede jacket with a quilted flannel lining, she had second thoughts about just walking into the main office of *Ohio Heritage* magazine. They'd likely think the women from Dennison were a little nuts, but it wouldn't be the first time she and Janet had been accused of that. Why not embrace it?

Kim had called a few minutes earlier. She needed to run some errands for her mother, so she wouldn't be joining them. Maybe that was for the best. Two gutsy women would be less intimidating than three.

Debbie picked up her gloves and walked to the front window to wait for Janet. Next to her, at waist height, stood the small artificial tree that had been the perfect size for the corner of her studio apartment in Cleveland. In the living room of her new house, it appeared dwarfed and a bit ridiculous. This room needed something majestic. Maybe something real, that actually smelled like pine.

Or not. The thought stirred a swarm of dormant memories. She and Reed, tasked to pick just the right tree for the student union. A still, cloudless night, the velvet sky sprinkled with diamonds. Snow crunching under their boots. Mittened hands clasped. Laughter. Playfully arguing over what constituted the perfect Christmas tree. Hot chocolate by a fire. A lingering good-night kiss...

The honk of a car horn banished the memories as quickly as they'd come. Turning her back on the out-of-place tree, she walked out the front door, locked it behind her, and took a deep, bracing breath of fresh, cold air. She would not allow her December melancholy to seep into time with her best friend. They were on a twofold mission—to find out anything they could about Dennison's competition for the "Heart of Ohio at Christmas" contest and to simply enjoy being together outside of work.

As she opened the car door, she opened her mind to an opportunity to live in the moment and leave the past behind. She slid in, fastened her seat belt, and said, "Let's do this."

Janet studied her face for a moment before backing out of the driveway but thankfully didn't comment on whatever she saw behind the not-quite-natural smile. "Food and fun await."

"I looked at the *Ohio Heritage* website. They close at five. I'm picturing a harried receptionist anxious to get home to her family who'll take our names and numbers and tell us they'll be in touch."

"I'm picturing something a little more positive." Janet gave a goofy grin that told Debbie whatever she said next was not to be taken seriously. "In my mind she's single with nothing to do on a Friday night, so we offer to treat her to supper at the Roscoe Barbeque Company, and she likes us so much she not only agrees to send out pictures of the bench but also puts in a good word for us to her boss."

Debbie laughed. It felt good. "In other words, bribery."

"Well, I suppose you could call it that. I prefer to think of it as having compassion on a poor, lonely soul."

As they drove west, they chatted about things that needed to be done at the café in the upcoming week. Peppermint mocha was such a hit that they decided to promote it daily until after Valentine's Day. The old-fashioned cake doughnuts, the kind served to servicemen and women in World War II by volunteers, had run out by one this afternoon. Janet would have to plan on making a lot more on the days the Christmas train ran. When they reached the end of the expressway and Highway 36 merged from four lanes into two, they started talking about a strategy for approaching whoever they'd be allowed to talk to at the publishing house. This time, a serious strategy.

"I think we need a subtle approach," Debbie said. "Let's tell them about the bench going missing and see if they come to the same hypothesis we did."

Janet nodded. "And if they do, then we go with Kim's idea of having them ask their photographers to be on the lookout for it."

"Right. We definitely want to avoid making them think we're blaming them."

"Absolutely. Before we say anything else, we need to gush about how excited we are that Dennison is included in their contest." Janet dipped her head toward Debbie. "You're a better gusher than I am."

"Wow." Debbie pressed a hand to her chest. "That's the nicest thing anyone's said to me all day."

"Oh, I doubt that. I heard Greg compliment your apron."

Debbie sputtered. "Did you hear what he actually said?"

"He said it was pretty. Or something like that."

"He said his grandmother used to have a pink apron kind of like it. Then he said it was pretty. Essentially, he told me I reminded him of his grandmother."

"Aw. Isn't that the sweetest thing? I bet he really, really loved his grandmother."

"At least now I know what he expects out of our relationship. His grandmother owned a bakery, so I guess he's just after me for the doughnuts and cinnamon rolls."

"Probably." Janet winked. "Ian fell in love with me because I was the only girl he'd ever dated who'd go trapshooting with him. The point is, it doesn't really matter what brings two people together. It's what you build out of it that counts. And you two have the potential for something amazing."

Debbie sighed. Hopefully, the rush of air from her lungs was quiet enough that Janet hadn't heard. She wasn't in the mood for another "your future can be bright and beautiful if you want it to be" talk. "Maybe," she said softly.

Silence followed for several miles, then Janet glanced her way and said, "I'm sorry if I get too pushy sometimes."

The apology was all that was needed to make her eyes sting with tears she refused to shed. After a few slow, calming breaths, Debbie felt steady enough for an honest answer. "I know this makes no sense after all these years. I know I should have 'moved on' long ago. I've been praying about it a lot lately, and I think God is showing me it boils down to fear. For the most part, my life has been wonderful. Other than the pressure at work, I enjoyed pretty much everything about my life in Cleveland, and moving back was an adventure I looked forward to. But…"

"Something's missing?"

"Yes. Maybe. And I know what it is, so you don't have to point it out. I want a relationship, and Greg is an incredible person. He's interesting and funny and a great listener. But what I had with Reed was the kind of stuff in fairy tales. He swept me off my feet, and I walked around with stars in my eyes and my head in the clouds. What if I never have that with Greg? What if we got married and I spent the rest of my life…disappointed?"

Janet didn't answer right away. Then a soft smile curved her lips. "You will be," she said.

"I will be what?"

"Disappointed. Just the way you would have been eventually with Reed." She took her right hand off the steering wheel and held it up to stop the words already forming on Debbie's lips. "Reed was wonderful. We all loved him. But he was human, and even though you dated a long time and knew him well, things change when you're together 24-7. The traits that initially attracted and drew you can become irritations. You see the chinks in his armor, and he sees you at your worst, on those cranky, eat-a-tub-of-ice-cream-all-by-yourself days." She put her hand back on the wheel. "That doesn't mean it isn't still amazing. It just means that it gets real, and 'real' involves some disappointment. If you go into it knowing that, with your eyes wide open and a plan to give him a pass when he disappoints and to talk through those tough times, your life together will be incredible."

Debbie spent the next mile or so contemplating those words of wisdom. "You're right. I know that deep down, but when I read through Reed's letters and look at our pictures, it's like entering a sparkly, happy, make-believe world. We're smiling in every picture.

His words are nothing but loving. I want to freeze that feeling. But I know it's not real." She suddenly thought of one her favorite books. *The Velveteen Rabbit*. "Real takes a long time."

Janet smiled. "Do you still remember the whole thing?"

"Maybe." She answered with hesitation, knowing what would follow. She'd memorized a passage from the popular children's book for a public-speaking class she and Janet had taken together in high school.

"Let's hear it."

"Seriously?"

"Seriously."

Debbie pulled in a deep breath. She could do this at warp speed. "Okay. Here goes. *"'Real isn't how you are made,' said the Skin Horse. 'It's a thing that happens to you. When a child loves you for a long, long time, not just to play with, but really loves you, then you become Real.'*

"'Does it hurt?' asked the Rabbit.

"'Sometimes,' said the Skin Horse, for he was always truthful. 'When you are Real you don't mind being hurt.'

"'Does it happen all at once, like being wound up,' he asked, 'or bit by bit?'

"'It doesn't happen all at once,' said the Skin Horse. 'You become. It takes a long time. That's why it doesn't happen often to people who break easily, or have sharp edges, or who have to be carefully kept. Generally, by the time you are Real, most of your hair has been loved off, and your eyes drop out and you get loose in the joints and very shabby. But these things don't matter at all, because once you are Real you can't be ugly, except to people who don't understand.'"

Janet blinked hard, and Debbie wondered if she was going to cry. "Thank you for humoring me." She took a shaky breath. "This is me meddling again, but I see the way Greg looks at you, and I'm pretty sure he's the kind who will love you even when you get loose in the joints and shabby and your eyes drop out."

With just the hint of a smile, Debbie answered, "I think you might be right. Guess I shouldn't be so afraid to find out."

"Get ready to gush," Janet whispered as she pulled open the glass door of Ohio Heritage Publications.

"And you get ready to foot the bill for barbecue for three."

"Deal."

As they entered the hushed lobby, Debbie pictured the frazzled young mom desperate for a break or the lonely young single with no Friday plans slouched behind a desk, and she put on her best smile. The muffled sound of keyboards clacking somewhere in the unseen distance played backup to the soft strains of instrumental music piped overhead.

Her first glimpse of the receptionist caused Debbie to miss a step and almost collide with Janet. The person fit neither of the pictures they'd constructed. For starters, she was a *he*. And he was not young. The man standing behind the counter in a perfectly pressed and filled-out charcoal-gray suit that was likely made of 100 percent Italian wool had thick salt-and-pepper hair and a white goatee. This was a man who never slouched on the job. Maybe not even at home on his own couch. This might be a man who never even sat down on the job.

As they approached, Janet gave an audible gulp. Debbie answered with an almost imperceptible, "Uh-huh."

"Good afternoon, ladies. Welcome to Ohio Heritage Publications." He nodded toward a gold nameplate on the counter. "I'm Terrance Aschauer. How may I help you?"

"Well, um…" Debbie still felt a bit off-balance. "I'm Debbie Albright, and this is Janet Shaw. We own the Whistle Stop Café in Dennison." She paused and was rewarded by a flicker of recognition.

"One of our finalist towns. So nice to meet you. I've been to Dennison. In fact, two years ago we had a four-generation photograph taken in front of your depot at Christmas. I was thrilled to find out Dennison was chosen. Do you have questions about the contest?"

Debbie folded her gloved hands in front of her. "In a way, yes. We read every issue of your magazine from cover to cover, and we're thrilled to be in the contest. Such an incredible opportunity to show off our nostalgic little Christmas-card town." If she was laying it on too thick, she couldn't tell by Terrance Aschauer's expression. "But we're actually here about just what you mentioned—family pictures taken at the depot." When the man's trimmed brows drew closer together, she asked, "Did you, by any chance, have your family photo taken on an old wooden bench?"

"Why, yes. My parents and my wife and I sat on the bench with our children and grandchildren all around us." He tipped his silver-streaked head to the side. "Why do you ask?"

"Because that bench went missing last night," Janet answered.

Mr. Aschauer took a step back. "And you think it's because of the contest?" His tone implied he was personally offended. Both hands rose as if he were warding off an attack.

"No!" The moment Debbie uttered the word, she realized she'd have to take it down a notch. "We have no idea why it's gone. We've checked with all the people in town who have the official right to order it removed, but none of them know anything. As you recall, it's a big bench, not something kids could easily haul off as a prank. We're just covering all the bases. There are a lot of possible reasons why someone might take it, but—"

"You think it could be one of your competitors in the contest." There was an edge of steel to the man's voice.

It was Debbie's turn to raise a defensive hand. "We're not blaming the magazine. Not for a minute. But would it be possible for you to mention this to your photographers just in case they—"

Movement behind Mr. Aschauer stopped her. A woman, likely in her sixties or older, in a form-fitting black dress with a massive silver necklace and large silver-ball earrings peeking out from dark auburn hair, rose slowly. "Is there a problem, Terrance?"

Terrance stepped back, eyes wide with what appeared to be fear. "No, ma'am."

Spike heels clacked on the tile floor as the woman approached. "I'm Meredith Montgomery, owner of Ohio Heritage Publications. I couldn't help but overhear. I can assure you, there will be no talk or intimation of scandal of any kind in connection to our magazine." She lowered a pair of black-rimmed, cat's-eye glasses and peered at Debbie. "I suggest you ladies return home and await the results of the contest."

CHAPTER FOUR

When the café closed at three on Saturday, Debbie stood at the front window and watched the Dennison Christmas train depart. The café had been crowded since eleven with people, local and from states away, starting their Christmas season with this tradition. She couldn't count the number of questions she'd fielded about the bench. Around one o'clock, Greg and his boys had stopped in for hot chocolate and she'd asked them to move one of the benches from inside the museum to out under the eaves so families could pose there for pictures. But it wasn't the same, and it didn't stop the questions.

She turned over the Closed sign then buzzed through her cleaning routine quicker than usual, pouring the last of the salted caramel syrup into a cup of black coffee and setting it aside for Kim. The window thermometer hadn't reached forty all day and had its sights on the midthirties for the rest of the weekend. Now was the perfect time to get home, put on her softest, comfiest sweatsuit, and curl up with old letters and memories she could wrap around herself like a security blanket to ward off the December chill.

And maybe, when she finished, she'd box up the letters and not look at them again. Until next year. Maybe.

Janet finished her tasks first. As she reached for her coat, she said, "Why don't you join us for supper? I'm going to try a new recipe.

We'd love your company. And some of your baking powder biscuits."
Her light and airy tone didn't match the concern on her face.

There was no point in pretending in front of her forever friend.
Debbie offered up a weak smile. "Thanks, but I'm good."

"Deb…" Just three letters, but they carried years of meaning and
a Grand Canyon's worth of understanding.

"I'm okay."

"I just wish…" Janet left the sentence unfinished, but Debbie could
fill in her blanks. *I just wish you weren't stuck in the past. I just wish
you could get over Reed. I just wish you'd start living in the present.*

Debbie wished for all of those things too. Sort of. She wished that
one morning she'd wake up and know deep in her heart that her time
of mourning had come to an end. She would no longer want or need
to reread the letters signed "Praying for you, my love," or visit the
grave where she knew he wasn't. But that day wasn't today.

Janet left, and Debbie grabbed Kim's coffee and locked the café
door before walking over to the museum side of the depot to say
goodbye to her friend. Only two people, a couple holding hands, still
occupied the vaulted-ceiling space that once greeted soldiers on
quick refueling stopovers.

Debbie lingered over the black-and-white photos that lined the
walls, even though she could describe each one without looking.
She wondered, not for the first time, what it would have been like to
have been born sixty years earlier. To witness firsthand the courage,
sacrifice, and resilience of those who served in the war and of those
who waited for them to come safely home.

After the couple took their purchases to the counter and Kim
rang them up on the vintage cash register, handed them a bag, and

wished them a Merry Christmas, Debbie walked across the room. "I'm heading home." She handed the coffee to Kim.

"You're the best friend ever." Kim took a sip and closed her eyes for a moment. "Delicious."

They'd touched base earlier that morning about what had happened at the publishing house and the calls Kim had made on Friday afternoon that had also resulted in dead ends. But there'd still been a few people Kim had said she wanted to contact, so Debbie asked if she'd learned anything new.

Kim shook her head. "I talked to someone from public works. He didn't have a clue. Ian told me about the green truck, and I've asked around about it. Two people said they saw it around town but don't know who owns it. Has Greg heard anything?"

"No. He called the other chamber officers, and none of them had any idea." Kim had been busy when Debbie left yesterday, and Debbie hadn't taken the time this morning to tell her about Harry's suspicions. It took her a couple of minutes to bring her up to speed.

"That seems unlikely. I know Michael. I've heard he's gone to counseling, and he's even going to church. People say he's a changed man. Still, I guess it's a lead to check out. In fact, let me try right now. Even though we already know the board didn't formally order the bench's removal, it's not out of line for me to talk to each member." She pulled out her phone and tapped on a contact. After a minute, she shrugged. "Voice mail. I'll try again later."

"We have a very short list of people who might have had a motive. I'm going to talk to Rita Carson and Doris Kimball." A thought struck her. "Your mother knows everyone." Centenarian Eileen Palmer was one of Dennison's oldest residents. In 1943, at the age of twenty, she'd stepped in to serve at the depot when the stationmaster was drafted. Though her recall of recent events could be fuzzy sometimes, she was a wealth of information about things that happened back then. "Have you told her about the bench going missing?"

"No. Though I'm guessing she's already heard. You know how fast news travels at Good Shepherd."

"That I do." Until his own recent retirement, Debbie's father had been the director of the assisted-living home.

Kim tipped her head to one side. "Pretty sure she hasn't hidden the bench in her closet, but there is something going on there. Lots of whispering behind hands with a couple of her besties that stops as soon I walk in the room."

"'Tis the season for secrets."

"I hope that's all it is. She and some of her friends just watched one of those movies about nursing home residents busting out and embarking on their final adventure."

"Oh my. But hey, they'll have my full admiration if they're scheming some big escapade. May we all be so feisty at that age."

Kim gave a weak laugh. "True. But wait until it's your mom zip-lining or scuba diving at a hundred."

A fire crackled in the gas fireplace. On the coffee table, next to Debbie's feet encased in fuzzy red socks, sat a clear glass Christmas-tree-shaped light filled with swirling, dancing, silver glitter. Next to the tree was The Box. Yet unopened.

She'd been doing this for almost two decades, but as she hugged a steaming mug of vanilla latte, she had the sense that something was different this year. Was it that she was in different surroundings? Was it Janet's "I just wish" words that kept circling through her head? Or was it a nudge from the Holy Spirit? She closed her eyes. "Lord, I know You want me to live with open hands. Am I clinging too much to the past? If these memories are keeping me from living in the moment, I..." But she couldn't finish the whispered prayer, couldn't say the words of surrender that a part of her desperately wanted to utter. Saying them would feel like losing a piece of her soul. It would feel like losing Reed all over again.

After another sip from her mug, she set the cup down and picked up the square white box that had once held the cake topper she'd ordered for their wedding. She'd given the little bride-and-groom figurine to a coworker who'd admired it. And then she'd attended her wedding but not the reception. She couldn't bear to see it, to hear the music and see the joy on her friend's face.

Looking back, it seemed selfish, but her friend had understood. Just as Janet had after her wedding when Debbie ran to the bathroom instead of standing in the receiving line with the other attendants.

She opened the first letter, the first one Reed had sent from boot camp.

> *Hey, sweetness,*
> *I miss you already. People say absence makes the heart grow fonder, but I don't think this poor heart could hold any more fondness. It was doing just fine right there with you.*

*I've made a few new friends. No surprise, right? I know my
extroversion sometimes drives you nuts, but being able to strike
up a conversation with a fence post is serving me well here.*

For the first time in all her years of rereading, Debbie stopped
at "drives you nuts." Janet's words came back to her. *The traits
that initially attracted and drew you can become irritations.* Had
Reed's extroversion really annoyed her? Well, maybe on occasion,
when she was ready to leave a social gathering and he was working the room, trying to accomplish his goal of meeting every
single person at the event. Even now, she could feel that edge of
irritation he'd banish with the smile he reserved only for her. But
after years and years...

She tried to picture what her life might look like now if she and
Reed were coming up on their twentieth anniversary. Would Reed's
gregariousness, his Type-A need for socialization, still be charming,
or would it have started to wear on her more introverted personal-
ity? While she always loved being with friends, she also needed
downtime in between, something Reed had never seemed to require.

Maybe Janet was right. Maybe she'd created a fantasy built only
on the good memories, a fairy-tale world that didn't need large doses
of grace to keep the spark alive.

Her phone rang. She thought she'd turned it off. Probably Janet
extending another dinner invitation. She reached for it, surprised to
see Betsy's name on the screen. Reed's mother. She'd moved to
Florida years ago. At first, their calls had been weekly, as they strug-
gled to support each other, but after a year or two it dwindled to
once every few months. Debbie knew why she was calling. The

twentieth anniversary of their shared sorrow was less than two weeks away.

Gripping the phone as if she could draw strength from it, Debbie answered.

"Debbie, hi, how are you?"

"Doing okay. How is sunny Florida?"

"Bright and beautiful. I'm calling because I've decided I need to come up next week. It's been a few years and, well, I just need to be there. I'll spend a couple of days in Cleveland, hopefully with you, and then I want to see your new house."

"W-wonderful!" She hoped Betsy wouldn't notice her hesitation. It would be wonderful. She'd always loved her almost-mother-in-law, the flamboyant woman with so many of her son's ebullient qualities. "It will be good to see you. I have a guest room just waiting for you."

"You're sure? I can always get a hotel room."

"Nonsense. Besides, it will feel much more like Christmas with you here to make pfeffernuss."

Betsy's laughter filled a bit of the empty space in Debbie's heart. "It would be my joy. And would you mind a little trip down memory lane? Besides the cemetery, I want to visit some of Reed's favorite spots. The Rock & Roll Hall of Fame, West Side Market, and maybe the art museum. And definitely that wonderful seafood restaurant."

Debbie closed her eyes against a barrage of memories. Reed, grabbing a plastic microphone in the Rock & Roll Hall of Fame gift shop and belting out "Blue Suede Shoes." Buying their cake topper at the Market. And, the one that made her fingers curl into her palms, the five-star restaurant where he'd first taken her hands in his and said, "I love you." How was she ever going to entertain any future thoughts now? "That would be...great."

"I knew you'd love it. I'll make my flight arrangements and let you know exactly when I'll be there."

"I look forward to it." *Kind of.*

After they said their goodbyes, Debbie shut off the ringer and set her phone face down. She tucked her feet beneath her and pulled a butter-soft throw over her knees. A sip of still-warm-enough latte brought her back to the place of nostalgia and fairy tales she'd started in. She continued to read.

> *The guy in the bunk above me is from Dayton. Funny how here where we're surrounded by guys from all over the country it feels like we're next-door neighbors. Somebody started call-ing us the Buckeye Boys. Have a feeling that's going to stick. So when I get back, you can be my Buckeye Girl. It's not—*

Someone knocked at her front door. She thought about not answering. Anyone she knew would have called first. But then she heard voices.

Greg's boys. And Greg.

Her heart stirred with a strange mixture of annoyance and anticipation. Part of her wanted to stay in her warm cocoon. The other part, strangely, welcomed the interruption. "Just a minute!" She shoved the letters into The Box and slid it under the coffee table then jumped up and pulled the door open.

"Hi." Greg stood bundled in his work jacket with a *V* of cable-knit sweater showing, gloves, and a fleece-lined leather aviator cap with the flaps down over his ears. He stepped inside. "Tell me you're feeling spontaneous. The boys decided we needed a tree. Now. I could use your tree-choosing expertise. And company." He turned toward the bare, miniature tree in front of her window. "And it looks like you could use the same."

Debbie stared at the sad little tree. With a deep breath and fierce nod, she said, "A tree. And company. Exactly what I need right now. I'll get my coat."

December 4, 1942

Margie walked out of the depot after nine on Friday night. She, Helen, Madeline, and Eileen Turner had just finished slicing twenty loaves of donated home-made bread and decorating dozens of gingerbread men for tomorrow. Esther had bowed out early for a date. Nothing unusual.

The night air was crisp and still, the sky peppered with stars. Margie looked up and said a prayer for Jesse. She'd sent the telegram, exactly as he'd worded it. What did it mean? Jesse and Andrea had developed what Jesse called "sort of a code" when they were young. Margie had tried her hand at deciphering some of their messages but hadn't succeeded. It wasn't the kind of code you could solve by finding a key. Instead, it involved eliminating unnecessary words and rearranging the ones that were left. She'd often teased her friends that they were more like twins than siblings born two years apart. "Sometimes I think you each have half of the same brain," she'd once said, probably at a time when she and her brother Dutch were staring at Jesse and Andrea with no idea what they were talking about. She'd read about studies done to test for extrasensory perception. While she wasn't sure there was any validity to it, Jesse and Andrea certainly had a form of communication between them that, in Dutch's words, "Just ain't normal."

Margie had tried to pull out the relevant words from Jesse's note. Father. Give. Gold ring. David King. Christmas Eve. Man. Can't be trusted. *She'd eliminated almost half the words but was no closer to figuring it out. Who was David King? She'd never heard Jesse or Andrea talk about anyone by that name. Was the message about a real gold ring, or was that code for something else? And was Jesse exaggerating when he said it was a matter of national security?*

Jesse and Andrea's father was some high-up official at the Ravenna Army Ammunitions Plant. But why wouldn't Jesse have called him directly? Why all the secrecy? She'd felt like a spy walking into the telegraph office. She knew the woman from church who took down her message. Mrs. Daly was likely to say something to someone. Margie had wanted to swear her to secrecy, but that would only serve to increase suspicion.

Breathing in the cold air tinged with a hint of ginger and cinnamon, she stepped off the curb and headed east then took a left on North Fifth. When she passed the house where Jesse and Andrea Blackwell and their parents had lived until just over a year ago, she stopped, letting herself reminisce. She and Andrea had met when they were five and their big brothers were in Cub Scouts together. So many memories. Memories that stopped when things heated up in Europe and the government decided to buy up thirty-three square miles of land in Portage and Trumbull counties, two hours north of Dennison, forcing two hundred and fifty families to relocate so the Ravenna Arsenal could be built. The Blackwells, on the other hand, because of Mr. Blackwell's army job, were moved to the area. And away from her.

With a sigh, she continued walking, once again reminding herself to let go of bitterness. War required sacrifice. After two blocks, she turned right on Grant and smiled when she saw the glow of the porch light. Her parents would have gone to bed, but even though she was just days away from her nineteenth birthday, her mother never failed to leave the light on for her.

Her legs felt heavy, far older than her years, as she walked up the steps...and froze when the rocking chair creaked and a shadowy form rose from the corner.

CHAPTER FIVE

*D*ebbie had assumed they'd be picking out a tree at the lot next to the grocery store. Instead, Greg drove out of town, stopping first at Floyd's Gas Depot. Floyd Marsh came shuffling out, wearing his iconic striped bibbed overalls and matching conductor cap. He wore a red bandanna around his neck. Floyd March was as much a Dennison icon as the depot itself. A newspaper article about his life hung in the depot museum. In his teens, he'd rebelled against his father, who worked for the McGarry Furniture Company, and instead of learning the art of furniture crafting, he'd opened his own gas station while working part-time for the railroad. Now, at eightysomething, he still ran the tiny full-service station that was a museum in its own right.

In front of the white brick building with a red tile roof stood an original Sunoco gas pump. Old tin signs plastered the wall around the front door, advertising Pennzoil and Champion spark plugs. Greg rolled down the window. The boys jumped out, as all local kids did— even those as old as Jaxon—to put pennies in the vintage gumball machine inside. Hammer, sitting in the middle of the back seat, whined.

"Git him a treat, boys. Bucket's behind the counter." Floyd peeked into Greg's open window. "That dog's spoiled." He grinned. "Good to see you, Greg. Miss Albright." He tugged on the bill of his cap. "Fill'er up?"

"Yep," Greg answered. "How's business, Floyd?"

Floyd inserted the nozzle into the tank then stepped back to the window. "Pickin' up. People like to be independent till the temperature drops."

Debbie leaned forward. "We appreciate you, Floyd."

"Thanks, ma'am. Say, I've been hearing a lot of kerfuffle about that old depot bench. What's your theory?"

"No idea yet."

"Hmm. This town needs a bit of mystery. Good for business, don't you think?"

That thought hadn't crossed Debbie's mind. But he just might be right. For a moment she played with the idea of contacting both local and statewide newspapers. But then common sense took over. They didn't need a bunch of amateur sleuths combing the town.

They said their goodbyes and left the station to the sound of the boys popping bubblegum bubbles in the back seat.

Greg headed northwest. Debbie rested her arm on the picnic basket on the seat between them. Her elbow bumped something. A small axe in a leather sheath. "We're cutting our own trees?"

"Is there any other way?" This from Julian.

"Well… I've never done it. But then, I also haven't had a real tree since about 1999."

"*Never?*" Jaxon's shocked exclamation earned him a reproving look from his father in the rearview mirror. Debbie pretended not to notice.

"I'm always up for a new experience." She'd said the words without really thinking, just like she'd said she needed a tree and company. Like curtains parting in a dark room, she suddenly realized she meant all those things. What she needed this year was exactly the opposite of what Betsy had suggested. She needed new experiences and new traditions. A Bible verse from the book of Philippians popped into her mind. *Forgetting what is behind and straining toward what is ahead, I press on toward the goal to win the prize for which God has called me heavenward in Christ Jesus.*

Press on. Maybe that needed to be her new motto. She'd find time over the weekend to stencil it onto a sign to hang next to her bathroom mirror.

"We have another tradition I probably should have asked you about." Greg glanced across the front seat with a sheepish expression. "Hot dogs and s'mores down by the Eastport Bridge after we get the tree. In this case, trees. You game?"

"Picnic in December. Something else I haven't experienced. But I'm definitely game."

"Cool." Julian said it under his breath, but she heard it. Debbie looked out the passenger-side window to hide her smile as they rode past expansive lawns, still green, that would hopefully be covered with snow by Christmas, if not sooner. Something else she was surprisingly ready for. The pristine whiteness of new-fallen snow.

"Hey," Jaxon said, "did you figure out who took the bench?"

Debbie shifted in her seat to look at him. "Not yet. Have you heard anything at school? One of our theories is that it might have been a prank."

"Oh, sure, blame the teenagers." Jaxon's exaggerated indignation made them all laugh. "Just because Adam Billings let a greased pig loose in the cafeteria at homecoming, and a bunch of girls hung Coach Thomas's swim trunks from the flagpole…"

It felt so good to laugh. She'd been planning an entire evening of melancholy, and now here she was embarking on a new adventure. *Keep them coming, Lord.*

"I heard something," Julian said. "Brad Carson said his grandmother hated that bench because it reminded her of Brad's grandpa, who ditched her."

Debbie grimaced and saw the same look on Greg's face.

"Julian." Greg shook his head.

"What? That's exactly what he said. They got divorced a long time ago, way before Brad was born, but then his grandpa showed up three years ago with another wife. So Brad has a stepgrandma, and she's really cool, way more fun than his other grandma. She's like eighty, but she takes him cross-country skiing and tubing on the river and stuff."

Debbie turned to Greg. His eyebrow rose. "Have you talked to Rita Carson yet?" he asked quietly.

"Not yet. Guess I'll put it on my list for tomorrow." She angled toward the back seat again. "Julian, did Brad think it was possible his grandmother had the bench removed?"

"I dunno. He just said she hated it. Hey, I bet I could get Brad to take me to her house and we could snoop around."

"Maybe she hid it in her garage," Jaxon added, "and whenever she gets mad, she goes out and smashes at it with a sledgehammer. Her own personal rage room. How cool would that—"

"Jax." Again, Greg silenced one of his boys with just his tone and a look. And once again, doubts assailed Debbie. Would she always feel like an outsider, left out of their years of shared experiences, unable to communicate on a level where tone of voice and the slight squint of eyes spoke volumes?

She swiveled even farther around. "We'll follow up on that lead, Jaxon. I doubt very much that Brad's grandmother felt so strongly about the bench that she got rid of it, but she's lived here a long time and might know something."

The half smile Jaxon quickly hid warmed her heart. She made a mental note to search for ways to validate the boys' opinions. When they weren't blatantly wrong, of course.

Greg turned right onto Wolf Run Road then pulled into a gravel driveway. A woman in a plaid flannel shirt waved from a side porch on the yellow farmhouse. Greg waved back but kept driving. The gravel ended, and he followed two worn ruts in the grass until they reached a spot where two other cars, one pulling a trailer, were parked.

When they got out, Hammer ran in circles, sniffing the ground and then the air, as if celebrating the freedom of the outdoors. Taking her cue from him, Debbie sucked in a deep breath, savoring the smell of pine on the cold air. "What are you looking for? What constitutes the perfect tree?" She aimed her questions at the boys.

Jaxon, taking the lens cap off of what seemed like a quality camera, didn't answer, but Julian grinned. "Stick with me. I'll show you the ropes."

"Don't listen to him," Jaxon said, snapping a picture of Hammer. "He likes Scotch pines. The needles are too long. All the ornaments fall off." Jaxon beckoned to her. "I'll find you the perfect tree. You need a Fraser or Douglas fir. The needles are just the right length, and they—"

"No way!" Julian retorted. "Those dumb little needles get stuck in your feet and…"

As the boys continued to argue, Debbie locked eyes with Greg's smiling blue gaze and felt, in this moment anyway, that she belonged.

Greg's SUV, now parked on a wide shoulder near the bridge, had three trees lashed to its roof. A towering Douglas fir for him and the boys, a seven-foot Fraser fir and a four-foot Scotch pine for her. One look at Julian's dejected face had convinced her she needed a tree for her bedroom.

Debbie listened to the swish of water over river rocks as she held a blue enamel cup close to her chin, letting the warmth seep through her gloves. She inhaled the rich aroma of hot chocolate "with a pinch of chili pepper like the Mayans made it," as Julian had explained. She leaned back in the canvas camp chair and let contentment wash over her like spring rain. Julian had made her a s'more, being careful to toast the marshmallow just the way she'd ordered—dark brown but not black. She'd had to turn down the next three offers. One indulgence of sweet, melty-chocolaty goo was enough. So she simply watched and laughed as Greg and his boys tried to sabotage each other's attempts at toasted marshmallow perfection while Hammer lay at Greg's feet, gazing longingly at each one in turn, silently begging for treats. Instead of feeling left out of the banter, she studied the boys, wanting to learn what kinds of things mattered to them and each one's brand of humor.

When the boys finally sat back, groaning and patting their stomachs, and Greg added another log to the fire, the first snowflakes of the season began to drift slowly down. Julian stuck out his tongue.

Jaxon grabbed the sleeve of his brother's jacket. "Don't move." He lifted his camera and zoomed in on a trio of individual flakes.

"Your dad says you've got a real eye for photography," Debbie said. "I'd love to see some of your pictures."

Jaxon shrugged. Debbie tried to think of another way to engage with him, landing on the age-old "How's school going?"

Jaxon shrugged again. "Okay."

Julian let out a loud sigh. "Horrible. Seventeen days until Christmas break. We have to write about somebody famous who was born in Ohio. I thought it would be cool to write about somebody who was born here in Dennison, who maybe went fishing in this same river or took the train from the same depot. I picked Walt Wait, the football player. He's the only famous guy born in Dennison, but Mr. Hendrick said Cassandra Davis picked him first."

"Clark Gable was born in Cadiz," Greg said. "That's only about half an hour away."

"Clark who?"

"He was a famous movie star back in the Golden Era of Hollywood. I understand he was quite a heartthrob and a bit of a scoundrel. Married to Carole Lombard at one point, as I recall."

"No thanks. I don't wanna write about all that romance stuff."

Debbie laughed at Greg's eye roll. "Does it have to be a guy?" she asked.

Julian's dimple appeared in his right cheek. "No offense, but I kinda want to write about somebody who did something adventurous or dangerous."

Debbie pressed her lips together to restrain a smile. And to keep from pointing out to the boy's father that he needed to do a bit of retraining concerning stereotypes. "So you wouldn't be interested in a silent film actress who starred in movies like *The Werewolf, The Girl and the Tiger, The Phantom Light, Our Enemy's Spy*, or *Cast Adrift in the South Seas*?"

Julian's mouth gaped. "Seriously? Can we get those on Netflix? She was born here?"

"Yep. Her name was Marie Walcamp. She was born in the late eighteen hundreds and went to school right here. She moved to New York to act on the stage then starred in her first film when she was nineteen. She eventually ended up in Hollywood and was in more than fifty films. They called her 'the Dare-Devil Girl of the Movies' because she did all her own stunts."

"Wow. Cool."

"Sadly, when her career started slowing down, she suffered from depression. When she was only forty-two she took her own life in her Los Angeles apartment. Since she made most of her movies at Universal Studios, they scattered her ashes over the back lot."

By the time she finished, more than the firelight sparked in Julian's eyes. "How come I never heard about her?"

"We have a picture and a short biography of her at the depot. But she died a long time ago, and people forget. She died in the thirties, so there wouldn't be anyone still living who'd remember her."

"But there might be someone whose parents knew her." Greg had been leaning back against a log behind him, clearly enjoying their interaction, but now he sat up, resting his elbows on his knees.

"It would have to be one of our oldest citizens," Debbie said. "Someone who grew up here. We could talk to Harry. Or..." She got an idea and felt her pulse quicken. "You know the phrase 'kill two birds with one stone'?" She looked from Greg to Julian and back again.

Greg's eyes widened. "Rita Carson. Brad's grandmother."

"She's the one who hates the bench, right? So…" Jaxon's excitement was evident in the way he tapped his fingertips together in a fast staccato beat. "If we go and ask her about the movie star, we can just casually mention the missing bench."

Greg nodded then opened his mouth to say something, but Julian beat him to it. "No. *They* can talk to her." He waggled a finger between his father and Debbie. "*We* can go snoop around in her garage and behind her house and—"

"Whoa." Greg laughed, but there was a warning in his tone. "There will be no trespassing."

Julian slouched like a deflated balloon. "Fine. But we can look around *in* her house. I mean, I'll probably have to go to the bathroom while we're there." His eyebrows wiggled comically.

"It just so happens, coincidentally, that I put her number in my phone yesterday." Debbie savored the expressions on the boys' faces.

"Call her now!" Julian pulled back his sleeve and looked at his watch. "It's only quarter after seven."

Debbie took out her phone and slipped off her gloves. "No time like the present, right?" She tapped on Rita Carson's number then put the phone on speaker.

"Hello?"

The word sounded more like a confrontation than a greeting. Greg shot his boys another silent warning as they both looked ready to laugh.

"Hi, Rita, this is Debbie Albright. I was wondering if—"

"I didn't take the stupid thing."

"Um...what?"

"The bench. Everybody thinks I took it. How, exactly, do you imagine I would manage it? Think I just popped on over in the middle of the night and tossed it in the back of my Audi? I'm an eighty-two-year-old woman, for Pete's sake."

Debbie stared at the phone, mind momentarily blank, feeling a bit like the kid who got caught opening the cookie jar. "Actually, Greg's son Julian is doing a report for school on Marie Walcamp. We were wondering if your parents knew her and if you could tell us—"

"Well, why didn't you lead with that? My mother knew Marie. And I've got stories about that girl that could curl your toes. I'm in my bathrobe and slippers, but come on over. Can you stop and get me a box of Fig Newtons at the convenience store on your way?"

Debbie looked at Greg, loving the mirth dancing in his eyes as he nodded. "Absolutely. We'll see you in a few minutes."

CHAPTER SIX

Rita Carson met them at the door wearing a plush pink robe and fuzzy teal slippers. She wore a satin cap on her head. A few curls peeked out, framing her lined face. "Watch your step," she barked. "That Kelly girl was making me a new threshold. Old one was all worn down. Don't suppose it'll get done now." The cap jiggled as she shook her head. She pressed a hand to her temple. "I go to bed early because I'm up at five for my morning constitutional." Debbie had a feeling that was both a way of explaining how she looked and a warning not to stay too long.

Debbie, Greg, and the two boys walked into a dark, crowded living room heavy with ornate furniture and brocade drapes that blocked out the light from the streetlamp in front of the Cape Cod-style house. The only illumination came from two table lamps coated with a layer of dust and the glow of an open laptop on the dining room table.

Rita took a wingback chair with scrolled wood trim surrounding tufted red cushions. Debbie imagined it sitting center stage on the platform of a majestic throne room then had to stifle a laugh as the little woman used an ornate cane much like a scepter to point to a love seat. If Rita's fifth-grade students had seen this chair, they would have likely called her the Ice Queen or Her Majesty the Warden instead of simply "the warden."

"Adults there," Rita commanded, and Debbie and Greg obediently sat side by side on burgundy and gold tapestry. The boys shared a piano bench Rita had apparently pulled out to accommodate them.

Debbie reached across the coffee table that separated them from the throne and handed the package of cookies to Rita. It was then she noticed the photo album on the table. It was open to two pages filled with black-and-white photographs and newspaper clippings of Marie Walcamp. Debbie angled the book so the boys could get a better look at the photographs that included studio head shots as well as pictures from some of her movies. They ranged from profile photos with sleek, coiffed hair to one where she stood barefoot in ankle-deep water wearing a leopard skin dress that came down to her knees. Wild, marcelled hair flowed freely past her waist. The caption beneath it read, *A Daughter of the Jungles (1915)*.

"Whoa," Julian said. "That was over a century ago."

Rita rolled her eyes. "Youth. So you want to hear about who she was before she made it big?"

"Yes!" Julian slid to the edge of the bench. "Please."

Greg smiled, clearly pleased his son had listened to the "Be polite no matter what" talk on the way over.

"My mother and Marie were inseparable friends before Marie went to New York when she was only sixteen. My full name is Rita Marie, named for the daredevil of the silver screen." She paused, and Debbie thought for a moment she might actually smile, but she didn't. "Mama had so many stories. In 1907, on Marie's thirteenth birthday, she dared my mother to climb up onto the roof of the train depot with her and sit up there all night long to watch the trains. And so they did...until they got caught by the stationmaster and were literally dragged home by their ears. Mama said it was one of the best nights of her life. And then there was the time..."

As Rita regaled them with story after story of Marie climbing water towers, swinging from hayloft ropes, and writing plays for neighbor children with lead roles for herself, Debbie studied pictures of the woman dubbed "the tragic serial queen." What had caused her to end her life? She married in 1920, but she and her husband never had children. Had she put all of her hopes for happiness in her career? If that was so, Debbie could understand why she sank into a depression when her acting opportunities began to dwindle. Debbie had experienced moments of loss and doubt after making the monumental decision to leave her career and move back home. Was she wrong to think she and Janet could run a café? Was she, like the dog with the bone in his mouth in the Aesop fable, looking at a mirage and leaving reality behind?

"...she just couldn't handle failure." Rita's final statement coincided with the thoughts in Debbie's head. But even if the café did fail, she had a support system of people who loved her, and her faith that would see her through the worst of times.

"That's sad," Julian said. "But she lived a really cool life." His gaze shifted to his father for a split second, and then he smiled sweetly at Rita. "May I use your bathroom, Mrs. Carson?"

Oh no. He wouldn't. Debbie felt Greg stiffen beside her.

Rita gave him directions to a doorway behind her and through a dining room that led to a hallway. Debbie cringed. Once Julian walked through the archway, they wouldn't know what room he actually ended up in. Rita's hearing still seemed to be sharp. Would she notice if he returned without the sound of water running or a toilet flushing?

"Excuse me. I forgot my phone in the car, and I want to look up more information." Jaxon stood and, without checking to see if his father gave approval, walked out the front door.

This was not good.

"There are more in there." After another story, Rita pointed at a manila envelope sticking out between the pages of the photo album. "One of my mother's friends sent them to her years ago. Her daughter collected memorabilia on Marie."

Debbie pulled out the thick envelope. It was postmarked 1952 and addressed to Doreen Eberhardt in Columbus. It had been slit cleanly along the top. She was about to pull out the contents when the name on the return address caught her attention. *Caroline McGarry.* "Was the woman who sent these related to the furniture company McGarrys?"

"Certainly was. Her husband started it, probably back in the twenties. When I was a child, they made all of their furniture by hand. They prided themselves on not using power tools. Furniture making almost came to a halt during the war, but sadly, sale of their other products picked up." She'd lowered her voice to a whisper, even though the people she was likely trying to shelter had both left the room. "They made caskets. Many were shipped overseas."

Debbie's chest tightened. "I remember reading about that. Like many companies, they had to hire mostly women. Imagine working there and then getting a telegram…" She left the thought unfinished. It triggered too many memories.

The tip of Rita's cane jabbed the air between them. "You lost a beau in combat, didn't you?"

At any other time of the year, she could have handled that question with only a twinge of emotion, but at the moment her emotions were too raw. "Yes." It was all she could manage.

Greg's arm, resting on the back of the love seat, lowered just enough for her to know that it was an intentional move. "How long have you lived here?" he asked Rita. Debbie would remember to thank him later for shifting the conversation away from her.

"Since I was five. My papa came home from the war, started working for the railroad, and built this house. When I got married my parents moved to Virginia to help care for my grandparents and gave us the house."

"Did your husband work for the railroad?" Debbie hoped it would be a subtle way to turn the conversation in a productive direction.

"Yes. He did." She spoke through clenched teeth. "He was a surveyor."

"That must have been an interesting job," Debbie said.

A glare answered her. "He traveled a lot."

"Did you ever go with him?"

"No. If I had, maybe…" Rita's hard gaze could have lasered holes in the front door. Debbie could imagine a younger version of the elderly woman sitting in the same chair, waiting, hoping her husband would return. The cane tapped the floor, the sound echoing in the silence. "And, so you don't have to ask, yes, he left me for another woman. And then another and another."

The distant flush of a toilet, followed by the trickle of a running faucet were the only sounds to break up the awkward silence that followed. Julian walked back into the room and took his place on the piano bench. His secretive smile amped Debbie's nervousness. "That's a cool Christmas picture of your family in the hallway, Mrs. Carson. Did you know Brad's my best friend?"

"I did not. Bradley is a fine young man." Her tone held shades of warning. Was she hinting that Julian had best not be a bad influence on her grandson? "My daughter insisted... We used to have a tradition of having our family portrait taken at the depot every year." Her smile, directed at Julian, was so tight Debbie wondered if her lips actually hurt. "I believe Bradley was nine when that one was taken." She gave a small wave, as if shooing away a pesky fly. "If you are interested, I can allow your father to take the album and make copies for your report."

"That would be awesome! Thanks!"

Rita stood, letting them know the short visit had come to an end. "You can see yourselves out," she said, then picked up her package of cookies, the ones she hadn't thanked them for, and shuffled slowly out of the room.

Debbie picked up the album and the envelope and, as directed, they let themselves out. As soon as the door shut behind Greg, Julian turned around, walking backward toward the car. "That picture! There's one at Brad's house. His family is sitting on the depot bench, and Brad's wearing the exact same Grinch pajamas, so it had to have been taken the same year. But Mrs. Carson isn't in the one at Brad's house. The rest of his family is there, but instead of her in the middle on the bench, it's his grandpa and his stepgrandma. She said Brad was nine, so that was three years ago. That's the year of the new grandma! I bet that's why Mrs. Carson said they used to have that tradition but they don't anymore. Because she got jealous of the new grandma and refused to do it again, and then she stole the bench so her cheating—"

"Whoa. Julian." Greg shook his head. "You don't know if any of that is true."

"Fine." Julian's sigh sounded frustrated, but his smile hadn't dimmed.

Jaxon met them at the car. "No sign of the bench in the garage. Well, maybe anyway. There was an axe and a pile of wood, like kindling. It looked like cut wood, not branches. So maybe—"

"Jax." Greg put a hand on his shoulder. "Let's rein in the speculation and stick to facts. Mrs. Carson did not hack the bench into kindling."

Jaxon laughed, and they all got into the car. When the doors were shut, Julian picked up where his brother left off. "Okay, so only the facts. We know Mrs. Carson didn't steal the bench. By herself. We don't know if she had somebody take it for her. We know there's an axe and a bunch of wood in the garage…"

While the boys went back and forth with their suppositions, Debbie took the envelope out of the album. Inside were at least a dozen newspaper clippings. And a letter. She pulled it out.

December 26, 1952
Dear Doreen,
Hope all is well with you. The garden club is not the same since you moved away. I have such fond memories of our

humble beginnings. *Thinking back on our first (and might I say pitiful?) victory garden, it's hard to believe it has been ten years. We have suffered much and learned much in those years, haven't we?*

You asked about my girl and the recent publicity. I'm afraid I can't answer any questions other than that she would say the paper's portrayal of her and Andrea as heroes is exaggerated. The tenth anniversary of their commendation was just a couple of days ago, so I suppose that's why it's come up again. She and her husband are living a quiet life in Ravenna with my adorable grandchildren.

With her blessing, I am sending you her old collection of articles about Marie Walcamp. I found them while cleaning a closet, and we both felt they would mean more to you. I'm sure you still miss your dear childhood friend. This life can be hard and leave us with so many questions, can't it? It does make us look forward to the day when we will live with our Lord without death or pain or shame or guilt.

How is your Rita doing? I do wish I had more advice on dealing with strong-willed children. I feel for you and the strain it is putting on your marriage. I have read that tenacious, independent children are most often highly intelligent. I hope that cheers you some. I pray daily for peace in your home.

Send me a note when you have time.

Love,

Caroline

"Learn anything?" Greg asked.

"Nothing that will help us, but it's interesting. Amusing, actually. Apparently, Rita was a strong-willed child."

Greg laughed. "Go figure."

"Dad." Julian used the exact tone of voice Greg used when reprimanding his boys. "That's not very kind."

Pressing his lips together to repress a wider smile, Greg glanced at his son in the rearview mirror. "No, it wasn't. I repent."

Julian chuckled.

Debbie looked at Greg. "You know all about this town. Do you know anything about a McGarry, a woman, who did something heroic?"

"Hmm… There have been so many McGarrys in Dennison. Why?"

"The letter mentions recent publicity about her and someone named Andrea. Evidently, they did something newspapers called heroic."

"Whoa!" The exclamation came from Julian. He held out his phone. "I just texted Brad and asked him if there were other pictures of him and his real grandma on that bench. Here's what he said: 'Nope. After my grandpa left, she burned every single picture of him, and after he showed up with Cool Grandma, she wouldn't go anywhere near that bench even though my mom begged her to keep our tradition.'" Julian slapped the back of the front seat. "I don't know how she did it, but I'm pretty sure we found the Bench Bandit."

December 4, 1942

"Andrea!" Margie gripped the railing as relief at recognizing the figure hiding in the shadows of her porch coursed through her limbs. Relief followed by confusion. "What are you doing here?" She should be at Kent State. Christmas break was weeks away. It took Margie a minute to have the presence of mind to rush to her friend and embrace her. It had been two months since they'd seen each other.

"We need to talk." Andrea's tone held the same sense of urgency her brother's voice had just three days earlier.

Margie gestured toward the chair Andrea had occupied before standing to hug her and then sat in the identical rocker next to it. "What's going on? Did you get the telegram?"

"I got it. When did you see Jesse?"

Margie told her about the phone call and meeting him at the depot. "What did it mean?"

Andrea let out a long, slow breath. "It's serious. You have to promise me you won't breathe a word to anyone of what I'm going to tell you."

"Of course. I promise." Margie scooted to the edge of the chair.

"You've met Barry Cunningham, right?"

Margie nodded. "The tall, Nordic-looking guy who worked with Jesse?"

"Yes." Andrea twirled a strand of dark hair around her finger, and Margie didn't miss the jagged, too-short fingernails. Andrea had stopped biting her nails years ago. What had caused her to return to the habit she hated?

"Jesse must have called him from the depot," Andrea continued. "For a few months now, Barry has been suspecting that someone working under my father is up to something. Files have been moved and are occasionally missing. My father is convinced it's all Barry's imagination, but now it looks like Barry found some proof that Jonathan Goldman, one of the engineers—"

"Goldman. Gold ring. Man who can't be trusted." Over the years, Margie had seen some of the coded notes Andrea and Jesse had passed back and forth, and she had always felt a bit left out of their "spy games." Now she felt like a little kid who'd just solved a riddle. But the importance of this one sobered her.

"Yes. There are several Goldmans working at the plant. That's why Jesse said—"

"David King's friend!" Margie interrupted. "King David's friend in the Bible was Jonathan!"

In spite of Margie's inappropriate display of the thrill at deciphering the clues, Andrea smiled. "Maybe now that Jesse's gone, you and I will have to share a brain."

Margie laughed. "Sounds dangerous."

Andrea's smile faded. "It definitely will be."

"What?"

"I need you to help me do something that could possibly put our lives at risk."

Margie felt her eyes stretch wide as a cold chill ran down her spine. Jesse's words, "national security," came back to her. "What do you mean?" she whispered.

"I need you to help me find out what Jonathan Goldman is up to. Whatever it is, I think it's going to happen on Christmas Eve."

CHAPTER SEVEN

*D*ebbie pushed back the same chair she'd occupied for count-less Sunday dinners since she was a child and stared out at snow-flocked pines framing the backyard. "That was fabulous, Mom." She picked up her dessert plate. "I need your recipe."

"I found it in one of the old *Ohio Heritage* magazines you gave me. It's called Potluck German Apple Cake. I've been looking for years for a recipe like my grandmother's apple cake. This comes the closest so far."

It wasn't the first time her mother had mentioned something she'd been doing "for years." It gave Debbie an unsettled, wistful feeling. Her mother had gotten the job at Trinity Health Systems and filled her free time volunteering at church. Her father had recently retired, but he kept busy with golf. While Debbie had pursued her career in Cleveland, life had continued in the house, and the town, she'd grown up in. Coming home wasn't quite as easy as she'd anticipated. "Speaking of that magazine…" She'd already told them about the conversation with Rita. Now she filled her parents in on Friday's road trip.

"It does seem possible that someone from one of the other towns could have done something," her mother said, "though I have to wonder what kind of person would care that much about a publicity opportunity for their town. And all the selected locations will be getting a lot of exposure leading up to the reveal anyway."

"Is there a prize for winning?" her father asked.

"As far as I know, a plaque and a spread in their online magazine, which is no small thing," Debbie said.

Her father took a sip of coffee, frowned, and set his cup down on a "Sunday saucer." "Has anything else gone missing? Seems like if anyone intended to sabotage our town, they'd be trying other things."

"Not that I know of. Not yet anyway."

Her mother mirrored Dad's expression. "Rita can be a difficult person, but I have a hard time believing she could, or would, orchestrate the disappearance of the bench, no matter how strong her motive. Maybe we need to look at the other side of the coin."

It took a moment for her meaning to register. "Doris?"

"She's as sweet as can be. Unless you cross her. I've seen her defenses come out in full force on occasion. It still baffles me why she and Rita had that much passion and energy about a piece of furniture."

Debbie laughed. She'd missed her mother's unique observations. "The bench represents memories." She thought of Rita burning her ex-husband's pictures. "Good and bad. Memories evoke emotion."

Her mother's hand slid over hers. "How are you doing? Really?"

"Okay. Most of the time. Starting to realize how silly I've been."

"Grief is not silly." This from her father, who'd lost his little sister when she was three years old and he was seven. A photograph of the smiling, towheaded little Debra hung in her parents' hallway. Like Rita, Debbie had been named in honor of someone whose memory was precious.

"I know. I'll never forget Reed, but it's past time I let myself be open to…whatever God has planned for me." She gave a tired smile. "That said, Betsy is coming to visit next week."

"Oh." Her mother's one word told of years of understanding. "Is she staying with you?"

"Yes. She wants to visit all of Reed's favorite places." She let her tone explain exactly how she felt.

Her father pushed back his chair and stood. "I'll leave you two to your girl talk." He picked up their empty plates. "Could you look at this as a chance to say a final goodbye? A healthy, letting-go kind of goodbye to some of the things that tether you to the past?"

Debbie stared at him. In truth, she was probably gaping at him. "My father, the wise old sage."

He narrowed his eyes, but they shimmered in amusement. "I will accept the wise sage label. Please retract the 'O' word."

She reached up to him, and he bent and hugged her then kissed the top of her head. "Thank you, Wise Sage. That is exactly the advice I needed."

"Well then," her mother said, "I suppose we don't need that girl talk after all." She looked at her husband, pride evident in her smile. "So I guess we should get back to solving a mystery. You know, there's a potluck at church tonight. And Doris Kimball has never been one to miss a free meal."

"Well then," Debbie copied her mother, "I suppose I'd better go home and whip up a dish to pass."

Debbie walked down the steps to the church basement, followed by Janet and Ian. None of them had planned on attending the potluck. Not until they'd heard it was one of Doris's favorite events.

"Mom's working in the kitchen," Debbie said over her shoulder. "She's going to invite Doris to sit with us."

"Good plan," Janet replied.

They set their dishes on the long banquet table in front of the kitchen serving window. Debbie had stopped at the store on the way home from her parents' house and bought the needed ingredients for lasagna. Wanting reinforcements, she'd called Janet. Her best friend, whose reputation as the Whistle Stop Café's amazing baker drew customers from miles around, had only needed to pull an unbaked apple pie out of her freezer. It was still warm, and the cinnamony smell had caused them all to groan on the ride to the church.

The first person Debbie recognized was Colleen Kelly. She sat alone at a table. Debbie told Janet she'd be right back and hurried over to talk to her. Colleen looked up and gave her a wan smile. "Hi, Debbie."

Debbie sat down next to her. "Are you sitting with someone?"

Colleen nodded. "My sister. She made me come, even though I haven't felt like eating since…"

"What's the latest on Ashling?" All she'd heard was that she'd sustained head injuries and the doctors were hopeful the surgery was a success.

"She's in an induced coma. They don't know"—her voice cracked—"what problems she might have…" She blinked hard and blew her nose on the tissue she'd been clutching in her hand.

"I suppose I don't need to ask how you're doing. This must be so hard."

Colleen nodded. "That girl is my world. This is…" She didn't need to finish the sentence. "We were supposed to be up in Ravenna, celebrating my parents' eightieth anniversary yesterday."

Debbie put her hand on Colleen's arm, a show of support when no words would help. When Colleen's sister returned with two plates, Debbie said she'd continue praying, offered to help in any way she could, and left the table, wishing she could do more.

As she joined Janet and Ian, her mother came out of the kitchen, wiping her hands on her apron. "So glad you're here. Doris is saving our seats." She winked and tipped her head toward the right side of the fellowship hall. Debbie glanced, as casually as she could, over her left shoulder. The short, round-faced woman in a flowered dress sat at the head of a table, presiding over it as regally as her nemesis had on her plush red throne, yet looking decidedly happier.

After a whispered conversation about logistics, they made their way to the table. "Hi, Doris." Debbie offered her widest smile. "Mom says you're saving seats for us."

"I am." Doris arced a pudgy hand across the table then greeted each of them by name as they sat in the order they'd predetermined. Janet and Ian on Doris's left and Debbie on her right with a space for her mother next to her. That left three open chairs. Debbie hoped whoever joined them wouldn't monopolize the conversation and compromise their mission.

"It's been a long time since I've seen you girls outside of the café," Doris said in her soft librarian voice, "except from my pew at church. I always sit in the back row, you know. When my rheumatism starts bothering me, I like to stand. Anyway, I still remember the years I had you two in Sunday school. So many questions!" She turned to Ian. "Does Janet still talk your ear off, wanting to know the 'why' of everything?"

"Oh. Aye." Ian's Scottish accent made itself evident every once in a while. "It's one of the things I fell in love with when we first met.

I knew I'd found a woman who wouldn't let me get away with anything."

Doris laughed and looked at Debbie. "And you, dear, any suitors in sight?"

Ouch. Debbie tensed and could see Janet and Ian doing the same. At that moment, three people approached their table. "Mind if we join you?"

Janet's laugh cut through the tension as she waved her hand the way Doris had, welcoming Greg, Jaxon, and Julian. She then turned to Debbie, and the irony of the moment was not missed. *Any suitors in sight? Maybe. Just maybe.*

Greg took the seat next to Debbie and, knowing full well her mother would be thrilled about this arrangement, didn't bother telling him she was saving it for her. "I didn't know you were coming," she said.

"Janet called," he muttered under his breath. "She thought the kids would want to be here."

Debbie was quite sure that wasn't all her friend had been thinking. She smiled at the boys, hoping the tinge of trepidation she felt at their presence didn't show.

"We had a talk on the way," Greg said, apparently sensing her unease. "They'll be on their best behavior." He reached across her, extending his hand to Doris. "Nice to see you, Mrs. Kimball."

"You as well, Mr. Connor. I hear good things about the way you're leading the chamber."

"I've got good people to work with. They make it easy."

"So, what do you think of our current crisis?"

"Crisis?" Greg echoed.

Doris looked at Ian. "Any leads yet?"

"Leads?" As if they'd strategized ahead of time, both men sounded equally clueless. Of course, Debbie thought, Doris might not be talking about the disappearance of the bench. After all, it couldn't exactly be called a crisis. Not yet anyway.

"You followed up on that gas can, right?"

Ian had likely been trained to keep his expression blank, but Debbie had known him long enough to know he was genuinely baffled at the moment. "What gas can?"

"The one they found in front of the depot after the bench disappeared."

Turning in his chair to give Doris his full attention, Ian said, "I haven't heard this. Start from the beginning, please, and tell me everything you know."

"Well…" Doris clasped her hands. Her eyes gleamed, and she appeared to be struggling to keep her usual librarian restraint. "My friend Vera's great-granddaughter cleans at the real estate office across the street from the depot. It was still dark when she went to work on Friday morning. Just before she turned into the parking lot, she almost ran over something. It was an old, rusty gas can. Anyway, she picked it up and put it in her trunk so she could maybe ask around for who lost it. It wasn't until the sun came up that she saw the bench was gone. She assumed it had been taken inside for the winter. She's new in town, you know. When she found out no one had a clue what had happened to it, she told Vera she wondered if the gas can had anything to do with the bench going missing. Vera said it looked like one her father had owned back in the forties. It was red, with one of those safety levers on the cap like they all used to have, you know.

Well, no, I suppose none of you would know. Anyway, I thought for sure she would have taken it to the police by now."

"Thank you," Ian said. "It's possible she talked to one of the officers and I just haven't heard about it yet. I'll look into it."

With all the buzz about the missing bench, Debbie knew it was doubtful a possible clue had been turned in without Ian knowing about it.

"I don't have the energy to fight for its preservation like I did years ago, but it's such a landmark, a symbol of all our community has endured." Doris glanced around. "And I think"—her voice lowered to her usual librarian volume—"we all have a pretty good idea who the most likely suspect is."

"Rita?" Debbie suggested.

"Oh no, dear. I mean, she's a close second, but think about it. Who in this town would still be using an eighty-year-old gas can?"

CHAPTER EIGHT

*A*s Debbie flipped the Open sign on Monday morning, she reflected on the weekend that hadn't turned out at all like she'd planned. Her anticipated time of quiet reflection and reminiscing had gotten so filled that she hadn't even had a chance to get back to The Box. Actually, she'd had the time last night after the potluck, but she'd chosen to put on pajamas and watch a Christmas movie instead.

She waited while she watched Harry slowly making his way along the sidewalk with his faithful sidekick. She opened the door then offered Crosby a piece of a doughnut from Saturday's batch. "I could set my watch by you two," she teased.

"Old habits die hard." Harry moved past her. "Every mornin', these old legs just bring me here, even 'fore I'm completely awake." He walked toward his favorite seat. "Did I ever tell you that I was fifteen when I started working as a porter?"

He had told her, of course, but she never minded listening to his stories, even the ones she knew by heart. "I think you did tell me that. Have I ever told you how grateful the whole town is for your years of service?"

Harry's deep brown eyes danced in the glow of the compliment.

"Pop Pop." Patricia stepped through the door. "You were supposed to wait for me." Her tone was gentle, but the concern on her face made her look stern.

He smiled at her. "I haven't taken orders from anyone other than the Almighty since I retired, and I don't intend to start now." He looked at Debbie. "We'll both have chocolate-covered doughnuts. See, I'm still the one calling the shots." Gripping the table, he lowered onto the seat.

When Debbie returned with two doughnuts and their usual coffees, one in a to-go cup, Harry said, "You know, I was thinking this morning about the day back in 1943 when that bench arrived. I was here to help unload it."

Debbie put her tray under her arm. "It came on the train?"

"Yep. Ordered by a soldier for his true love. That big heart with the initials that's right smack in the middle was already on it."

"You should talk to one of the O'Sullivans," Patricia suggested. "Their family came here after the potato famine in Ireland, all miners and railroad workers. Pop Pop has told me so many stories about working with them. They've got photo albums and diaries going back before Dennison was officially a town. I'm sure they have information from the forties."

"Good idea. Carly O'Sullivan came in on Friday. She was practically in tears when she saw the bench was gone. They've been having family portraits taken there as long as I can remember. I think her great-grandma is still around." Debbie cringed inwardly at her choice of words. But Harry's expression seemed to show something else. She couldn't explain it, but she got the impression he was hiding something. Maybe it was just all the talk of the missing bench. Her suspicious nature was in overdrive.

"Yes. Madeline O'Sullivan." Patricia looked at Harry. "She's living at Good Shepherd, isn't she?"

Harry took a sip of his coffee. "Yep. She's a couple years younger than me, but she's still got her wits about her and dresses like she's fixin' to walk down a runway." He turned to Debbie. "Have you talked to Eileen?"

"Kim said she'd talk to her. I haven't heard anything yet. So the bench was ordered by someone whose initials were MM or JB."

Harry nodded.

The bell above the door jingled, and two brothers, friends of Jaxon and Julian, came in for their usual eat-on-the-way-to-school breakfast. Janet was on the phone, so Debbie excused herself and met them at the pastry case. They pointed out their selections "Milk and cinnamon rolls coming right up." Then she called to Harry. "Noah and James are here to talk about the work you used to do after the war right here around this depot." James had inquired previously about when Harry would be around, saying he needed information for a school project.

James glanced at his smartwatch. "We've only got twelve minutes, Mr. Franklin. But could we get started?"

"Here, take my seat," Patricia said. "I'm off to work." She rose, picked up her cup and the doughnut she'd only taken a bite out of, and kissed her grandfather's cheek. "School 'em, Pop Pop," she said.

"I intend to do just that, young lady." Deep brown eyes glinted with mirth. "Well, boys, I don't necessarily recommend working as hard or as long as my friends and I did during the war, but let me tell you about it."

The boys sat across from him, and Debbie looked at her watch. She realized it might be up to her to make sure his history lesson didn't spin past twelve minutes.

"You see, way back, just after the Civil War, a man named George Pullman hired formerly enslaved African Americans to work as porters. The Pullman Company was a separate business from the railroad lines. It owned and operated sleeping cars that were attached to most long-distance passenger trains. You've probably toured the Pullman cars here at the station. Those trains were kinda like a chain of hotels on wheels. Our job was to carry passengers' bags, shine shoes, send telegrams for them, change sheets in the sleeping berths, serve food if the train had a dining car, and anything else people wanted us to do.

"My father was a porter, as was my granddaddy. I don't recall ever wanting to do anything but work for the railroad. We worked long hours and weren't always treated with the greatest respect. 'Course, things were a bit better for me than for the men who came before me. Porters weren't paid much, but it was one of the best jobs available for African American men back then. By the time I came along in 1943, even though I still had to endure a tremendous amount of prejudice, things were a little better because of the Brotherhood of Sleeping Car Porters, which I was a member of. The organization helped us get better working hours and higher wages.

"The job taught me the value of good, honest work. Met some famous people too. The most memorable was Jackie Gleason. Don't suppose you've ever heard of him. He was a comedian. Had his own

TV show. Big, big man." Harry curved both arms away from his body. "Just like Santa, his whole belly shook when he laughed. It was in 1956. I was a conductor by then, and everybody was buzzing about who was going to get to see Jackie Gleason. He was on his way to Florida. Brought his own piano. Can you believe that? His car was hoppin' with music and dancing. I came in to collect tickets, and he stopped playing, held out his hand, and asked my name. He did that with everyone—called them by name no matter what color their skin was. That would have been enough, meeting a famous guy who treated everyone with respect, but that man took it one further. He gave every porter and conductor a hundred-dollar tip."

"Wow." Both boys spoke in unison.

"Today, that'd be more than a thousand dollars. So, if ever you need a reason to persevere at a job, remember my story. You never know when you might meet someone famous, or just someone really kind and generous. Makes you want to be like him, doesn't it?"

James nodded. "Sure does. But I don't think anybody famous is going to show up for pizza at Buona Vita where Noah works."

A sly smile created ripples in Harry's copper-colored skin. "Ah. That's where you're wrong. Did you know that establishment has been around since about the time your grandparents were born? I remember the year Neil Armstrong, first man to walk on the moon, walked into Buona Vita…" Harry looked at his watch. "Well, guess our time's up."

The boys groaned, and Debbie handed them each a white bag and a to-go cup. "Harry's here this early every morning, boys. Guess you'll have to come back."

"Guess so," James said. "I have to write a story on somebody famous who left a legacy in Ohio."

Harry's laugh filled the café. "I'm no famous person, but if it's stories you want, I've got 'em."

The boys laid down their money and said goodbye. Debbie picked it up and almost yelled after them, but then she realized what had just happened.

Noah had left her a five-dollar tip for a sweet roll and milk. Resting her hand on Harry's shoulder, she said, "You may not be famous, Harry, but you're sure leaving a legacy."

By ten, the café started to empty. The calm before the storm, as Janet often called it. The lunch crowd would start filling tables at eleven. Debbie picked up her now-cooled half cup of sugar-and-spice coffee and stuck it in the microwave. When the bell dinged, she hugged the bright red mug, savoring the mingling of cardamom, allspice, ginger, and cloves sweetened with maple syrup. It was a new recipe, and customers loved it. "I found out something interesting about the bench from Harry this morning." She spoke to Janet's back. "The heart with JB and MM was already carved on it when it arrived here in 1943."

Janet turned around. "So maybe it was ordered that way? That would explain why it doesn't look hand-carved like all the rest."

"And it probably means that either JB or MM ordered it. Patricia suggested we talk to one of the O'Sullivans. And we haven't heard if

Kim talked to her mom yet. Oh, and then there's Floyd. That eighty-year-old gas can is a pretty straight arrow to him."

"I can't let myself think that sweet man had anything to do with stealing the bench." Janet gave a sigh. "But I guess we can't leave any stone unturned."

"I don't want to consider it either, but I keep going back to something he said about a mystery drawing attention to the town and that it would be good for business."

Janet stopped sprinkling powdered sugar over a tray of jelly rolls. "He said that?"

"Uh-huh."

An uneasy silence followed. Floyd had been friends with Janet's grandfather, and she'd always called him Uncle Floyd. Debbie needed to dispel the gloom. "I'm going to stay late to finish decorating. Want to help?"

It seemed to take Janet a moment to switch gears. After a few seconds, she set the shakers down and brushed her hands on her forest-green apron. "Yes. Ian's working until six, and we're having the leftover pot roast we didn't eat last night. Why don't you join us for supper? Then we can work until six if we need to, and you won't have to think about making food." She gave a look Debbie could only describe as a hopeful grimace.

"I would love to. Thank you."

"You seem…happier?" Not just an observation. Janet had turned it into a question.

"It seems the Lord wasn't pleased with my pity-party plans for the weekend, so He messed them up with all sorts of fun stuff." She filled Janet in on all of her welcome interruptions, knowing that hearing she'd spent time with Greg would only strengthen her friend's conviction about her "big, bright, handsome, blue-eyed future." With a sigh she admitted, "I'm reluctantly coming to the conclusion that maybe it's okay to be happy in December." Peering over the edge of her mug, she restrained a smile as she watched a very big one spread across her best friend's face.

"Then I will do everything in my power to support that conclusion." Janet's eyes danced, a look that could only mean trouble. "How about I come over and help you decorate that giant tree of yours tomorrow after work, and then on Wednesday we can go Christmas shopping, and on Thursday we can bake gingerbread cookies and—"

"Don't push it." Debbie laughed, beginning to feel like the person she was the other eleven months of the year.

"But I didn't even get to the caroling part. And then there's eggnog and fruitcake and gingerbread houses. I bet Greg's boys would love to get in on that. And afterward we can invite some people for a party at your house. I saw a recipe for white chocolate peppermint fondue that would be just per—"

Debbie held up a hand. "In spite of my new conclusion, I still reserve the right to a few sackcloth-and-ashes days."

"Fine. You go ahead and plan those. But God and I are going to have a talk about continuing to interrupt them."

December 11, 1942

"I'll be back tomorrow night," Margie assured her mother for the second time as she rolled a blouse to fit in the corner of her overnight bag.

"This is just all so…unexpected."

Andrea smoothed the covers on the twin bed she'd slept in. "I'm sorry I surprised you this morning, Mrs. M. I simply had to see my best friend. Man troubles, you know."

Margie looked away. Andrea was far better at this game of subterfuge than she was, and she knew her lack of skill would show on her face.

A small smile tugged the corners of her mother's lips. "I'm not so old that I don't remember how that feels. Nothing better for a troubled heart than time with a dear friend. Just be careful on the bus. That's a long ride, and you can't trust people these days."

If her mother only knew the accuracy of her words. "We know, Mom. We're worldly-wise girls now, you know." Margie closed the bag and pecked her mother's cheek.

"One year of college does not prepare you for the evils of this world." Her mother twisted her apron. "Call us when you get there. Please? Call collect."

"No need to reverse the charges, but I'll make sure she calls, Mrs. M." Andrea kissed her other cheek. "Thank you again for breakfast. I've dreamed about your bacon waffles since we moved." And then, in true Andrea fashion, she wrapped her arms around the woman who had been her second mother since kindergarten. "I've missed you so much."

Ten minutes later, Margie waved at her mother, who stood on the porch dabbing her eyes with the hem of her apron, and she and Andrea began their walk to the bus stop. "Man troubles, huh?" She looked at Andrea and shook her head.

"I did not lie."

"No, you didn't. So, what's our plan? You said you needed time to sleep on it."

"I think I'm going to introduce you to Jonathan and his girlfriend."

Margie pressed her free hand to her middle, where butterflies cut a rug to the beat of her pulse. "O-kay. Then what?"

"Then you will become their best friend."

"But..." So many words could follow that one. "But they already know you. Why me?"

"I'm the boss's daughter. They might get suspicious if I suddenly want to be buddy-buddy. But if I throw a spontaneous party tonight and invite some people from school and some from the plant, and you just happen to click with Jonathan and Laverne, it would be only natural that I'd be included when you come up to socialize with them every weekend."

"Every... I can't afford that."

Andrea grinned like the Cheshire cat. "Like I said, I'm the boss's daughter. We get military-issued bus passes."

"Oh. Good." Margie suddenly fixated on a word that had passed her by. She pictured a butterfly picking up drumsticks and adding a bass beat to the rowdy party in her stomach. "T-tonight?"

"Yep. We'll get you all dolled up, and then you just flash that Margie smile, and we'll be cookin' with gas."

Margie sighed. Only Andrea could make spying on a possible saboteur sound like a night of frolicking fun.

CHAPTER NINE

*A*fter leaving a voice mail message for Carly O'Sullivan, Debbie stepped out of the café. On her way to the storage room to pick up the artificial tree they'd bought a month ago, she was surprised to see Kim standing behind the counter. The museum was closed on Mondays. She was watching an older gentleman who was looking at model trains for sale. He must have made an appointment. Kim waved at her. "Need something?"

"Just going to get our tree. But I'd like to see those ornaments if—"

Kim held up one finger as the man approached the counter. Debbie nodded. A few days earlier, Kim had mentioned a box of vintage ornaments they could use. She wanted to check them out with Janet.

As she waited for Kim to finish the conversation, a new display caught her eye. The heading at the top of the board said DENNISON DEPOT'S FAMOUS BENCH THROUGHOUT THE YEARS. Kim hadn't mentioned putting it together.

The exhibit started in 1946 with square, black-and-white photos featuring couples and families posing on the bench. Debbie studied the women wearing belted coats with padded shoulders, gloves, smart little hats, and chunky heels. Men in fedoras, ties, and creased, cuffed pants. Boys in baseball caps and bomber jackets and little girls with pin curls and babies wearing blanket sleepers. She'd often thought that if she had a time machine, this would be the era she'd return to.

Turning her attention to the bench, she scanned the progression of carved dates and initials, stopping at a picture of a happy couple in 2004, two years after she and Reed had sat there, late one crisp mid-December night. The streets had been empty, and the sky spattered with stars. "I'm thinking we should start making some plans for next Christmas," he'd said. "I know it's a long way off, but there's something special I thought we could do to celebrate."

She'd thought it a bit strange that earlier he'd suggested spending most of his leave in her hometown instead of staying in Cleveland where their mutual friends were or with his mother in her Strasburg home half an hour north of Dennison, but she hadn't been at all prepared for what was about to happen. Lost in the moment, savoring the warmth of his arm around her but fighting tears at the thought of him leaving the next day, headed back to Afghanistan, she'd distractedly said, "What's that?"

Without warning, he got up and dropped to one knee. His hands went in his pockets, and he pulled out two boxes, one small, square, and black, the other rectangular, about the length of the palm of his hand. He held out the square one. "If you decide to keep this, you can have the other one."

Not breathing, hands shaking, she took the box and slowly opened it. Blue satin. And a marquise-cut diamond in a silver setting. A gasp, tears, and then she'd sputtered, "Of course, I'll keep it. And you." He slid it on her finger, and she fell into his arms, kneeling beside him. It was a long moment before she remembered the other box. "What's in that one?"

"Only one way to find out." His eyes gleamed like they reflected the starlight.

She lifted the lid and another gasp, this time mingled with laughter, broke the silence around them. A jackknife. With their names burned into the white ivory handle. She knew immediately what it was for.

They'd chosen the spot together. On the back, bottom-left corner of the bench. They took turns, on their knees, carving. She could see their initials now, in the picture of the smiling couple.

As if on cue, her phone vibrated with a message from Betsy. WILL LAND IN CLEVELAND 4:15 FRIDAY. I HAVE A RESERVATION AT A HOTEL FOR TWO NIGHTS. TWO QUEEN BEDS. LOVE TO HAVE YOU JOIN ME, BUT IF THAT DOESN'T WORK, I'LL RENT A CAR AND SEE YOU ON SUNDAY.

She hesitated before answering. She had no legitimate reason to say it wouldn't work. Would Betsy understand if she said revisiting all the places where she and Reed had made memories would only feel like opening wounds that were healing a bit more each year? But then she remembered her father's words. This was an opportunity to start fresh, to reflect on good memories before turning to a new page in her life story. She sent a quick text to Paulette Connor, Greg's mother, asking if she'd be available to work at the café on Saturday. She got a response in seconds. ABSOLUTELY!

She typed a reply to Betsy. LOOKING FORWARD TO IT. WILL PICK YOU UP AT THE AIRPORT.

"I'll help you find the tree." Kim approached from behind. "It might be buried. There's a string of bubble lights in the box I told you about and half a dozen of those clip-on glass birds with feather tails." She gestured toward the bench display. "What do you think?"

"I love it. Great idea. Besides just being a walk down memory lane, it could spark some conversations that might lead us to our Bench Bandit. Harry said the bench arrived on the train. Do you know who commissioned it?"

"No. I don't think I've ever found any info on it. Why?"

"Harry said he helped take it off the train. I'd always assumed it was made here at the McGarry factory. He said this"—she pointed at the center heart—"was already on it."

"Hmm. Interesting. Another thing I need to ask Mom about. She didn't have any information about the bench, by the way. There's a lot of speculation going on at Good Shepherd, but I don't think anyone there knows anything."

"How's your mom doing? She hasn't mentioned jumping out of a perfectly good airplane or swimming with dolphins yet, has she?"

"Not yet. But there's still something strange going on there."

After pulling another ornament out of the box Kim had given her, Debbie handed it to Janet. "What would you think about using only vintage decorations?"

Janet held the handblown glass wreath up to the light. "Why not? These are stunning. Maybe we should go all-out retro and string popcorn and cranberries."

Debbie almost laughed then stopped. "I love that idea. We could make a bunch of popcorn and invite some people to help. Old

Christmas carols playing in the background, hot cocoa and cookies…"

"Wait. Did my friend Debbie Albright just suggest something that sounds remarkably like a *Christmas party*?"

"Of course not. Not in the sense of being merry and bright and all that. This would be a practical gathering, solely for the purpose of decking the halls."

"Mm-hmm. So instead of inviting friends for a fun party, we're conniving them into working for us."

"Exactly." Debbie busied herself unwrapping another ornament. It was the only way she could keep a straight face. "We could even get them to do stencils on the windows with soap flakes like they used to do and make construction-paper chains to hang around the ceiling. There will be no fun involved."

"Sounds like quite an evening. But I can't be part of duplicity. We have to be up-front about it." Janet pulled a pen out of her pocket and pretended to write. "You are cordially invited to a non-party. Please do not wear red and green, and leave your Christmas cheer at home."

Debbie laughed then held up one finger as Janet's words sparked an idea. "What if we did just that? We'll host a Grinch party to find out who stole the symbol of Dennison's Christmas spirit. We'll invite the whole town and then mingle, trying to figure out who had motive and opportunity."

For several seconds, Janet stared at her as if she'd lost her last marble, then one eyebrow rose, followed by the other. "How deliciously Agatha Christie. All the suspects gathered in one place." She rubbed her hands together. "We'll serve Who pudding and roast beast."

"The *Ohio Heritage* photographer is coming on the sixteenth. What if we have it then?"

Janet looked at her like she'd lost more than her last marble. "Why?"

"Publicity. Like Floyd said, drawing attention to our mystery could be good for business. And our party will show the *Ohio Heritage* people how much we value our Christmas traditions."

"Okay. I'm getting your vision."

Debbie reached behind the counter for a pad of paper and held out her hand for Janet's pen. "I'll make up some flyers tonight. What do we want on them?"

"We have to have an ugly sweater contest."

"Definitely." Debbie wrote it down. "How about a separate prize for the best Grinch and Who costumes."

"Love it."

Another light bulb flashed in her brain. "What if, at the party, we announce a reward for the person who finds the bench? We'll have to charge, of course, so if we can keep the cost of the meal down and charge maybe five dollars a head extra, that can be the reward money."

"Why, again, are you not working in public relations? You're a publicity guru."

Debbie swept her arm in a wide arc. "What do you call this if not public relations?"

Janet laughed. "True."

"But since we're talking about publicity, there's someone we need to talk to, and the sooner the better."

"Floyd." Janet sighed.

Debbie nodded. "He knows you. Would you be willing to find out if he had anything to do with it?"

"I…guess. It'll be awkward, but I'll try." Janet glanced at the clock and let out another sigh. "Let's go get some gas."

Debbie took both of their coats off the coatrack. She picked up the pad and pen and asked, "What should we call the party?" as they walked out. Anything to keep Janet's mind off the uncomfortable task of questioning her old friend's integrity.

"How about the 'Who Stole Christmas? party'?"

"I like it." Debbie got into Janet's car, fastened her seat belt, and wrote the title at the top of the page. "December 16. Five o'clock? We could do a buffet line in the café but eat in the waiting area."

"We could maybe fit eight round tables, so instead of advertising to the whole town, maybe we need to just promote it at the café for our regulars."

"And our suspects," Debbie added. "Oh! Remember the scene in the movie where all the townspeople follow the Grinch singing 'God Rest Ye Merry Gentlemen'? We need a flash mob!"

Janet's withering look was comical. "Let's talk about that for next year."

"Fine. But I'm serious."

As they neared the gas station, Debbie pointed at a car pulling out. "That's Patricia." She waved as the car passed them.

"Harry's probably here to play chess," Janet said.

"I think I need a pack of gum." Debbie opened the car door just as Floyd walked out of the station. She greeted him.

"We meet again," he said. "Did you find the perfect tree?"

"Two, actually." She nodded toward the building. "Do you still carry Beemans gum?" She'd been thrilled when, five years ago, the gum she'd loved as a kid was back on the market.

"Sure do. Only place in town."

With a nod, she passed him and walked through the red-painted door with a round window in it. It had been years since she'd been inside the station, but everything looked exactly the same. She had a feeling that, even though the brands of snacks and soda were probably different, not much else had changed since Floyd took ownership.

A couple of steps in, she heard voices. Two men. Her line of sight was blocked by a life-size vintage cutout of race car driver Richard Petty, but she assumed they sat at the small square chess table in front of Floyd's potbelly stove. One voice was Harry's. She strained to recognize the other one.

"...think Madeline took it. Remember how we got your ugly mug in there? We gotta include that one." She knew that laugh. Pete Kimball, Doris's father. He'd been the elementary school custodian for decades. Doris's mother had held the same position Doris had recently retired from. Debbie's mother had told her stories about the gossip that had spread through town "like a horde of locusts" when the librarian fell in love with the janitor.

"Absolutely," Harry answered. "Soon as we get the bench back where it belongs."

"I'll talk to Eileen and see when—"

The door flew open, and Floyd practically stumbled inside. "Find the gum?" he yelled. What was he doing following her instead of pumping gas for Janet? And why did he sound like he'd just run a marathon?

"Not yet. I was"—Debbie scrambled for something plausible. And then she saw the row of little ceramic houses in the window— "admiring your Christmas village. I remember looking at it when I was about six years old."

"Yep. I've been setting it up for almost sixty years now."

Why was the man talking so loud? He'd appeared almost panicked when he came in. Debbie studied him. Thankfully, his breathing was slowing and he didn't seem to be in distress.

"Guess I'll go finish. Gum's on the house." He gave her a lopsided grin. "Christmas, you know." Before she had a chance to stutter a surprised thank-you, he was out the door.

Now that her presence was no longer a secret, she stepped around Mr. Petty as casually as she would if she hadn't just been eavesdropping and waved at Harry, who sat facing her. "Who's winning?" she asked.

"He's cheating." This came in stereo as both men pointed and laughed.

"Any leads on the missing bench?" Pete asked.

"Not much to go on yet."

"What's that?"

Debbie repeated, a bit louder this time, then added, "What do you think happened to it?" *And what were you about to say when Floyd walked in?*

Pete shrugged. "Most likely aliens."

"Wish they'd taken you instead of the bench," Harry answered. "That bench was a good listener. You can't hear squat."

"Good thing they didn't abduct you," Pete shot back. "They'd get the wrong idea of what normal humans are supposed to look like."

"Yeah, well…"

The banter continued, and Debbie suddenly felt like she'd stepped onto a movie set in the middle of filming a scene from *Grumpy Old Men* or *The Odd Couple*. She couldn't put her finger on it, but something was afoot. As she laughed along with them, she didn't miss the looks the two men exchanged.

They were up to something.

CHAPTER TEN

You're sure they said exactly that?" Janet asked as she turned the car onto the road.

"Yep. When I walked in, Pete was saying, 'Madeline took it.' Then Harry said, 'Soon as we get the bench back where it belongs.' Doesn't that sound like they have it? How else could they get it back where it belongs? Did you learn anything from Floyd?"

"Not a thing. Unless you count a gut feeling that he knows something. Before he got halfway to my car he yelled for me to wait a minute, and then he ran back inside. I mean, for a man his age, I'd call it running."

"He was out of breath when he came in and was practically shouting, like I was the one who was almost a hundred and didn't have the wherewithal to find the gum. He—" Debbie's jaw dropped as realization registered. "He ran in to warn Pete and Harry. He knew what they were talking about, and he didn't want me walking in on their conversation."

"That sounds very conspiracy theory-ish, but you could be right."

"What did he say when he came back out?"

"Something that didn't make sense at the time, but I get it now." Janet gave a slow nod. "When I handed him the money, he asked if we were headed out of town. He squinted at me, like he was suspicious

WHISTLE STOP CAFÉ MYSTERIES

of us being there. I think he was trying to find out why I was filling up when I only needed five gallons of gas. He got me so flustered I just couldn't come right out and accuse him of taking the bench."

"He's onto us. He knew we were there to talk to him. Or maybe he thought we knew the other grumpy old men were there and we were spying on their meeting."

"Which you were."

"But it wasn't premeditated. It will be from now on though. We need to be tracking their whereabouts whenever we can. Do you think Ian would help? Unofficially, of course."

"I'll ask."

Debbie replayed the men's conversation in her head. She'd forgotten to tell Janet one thing. "Right after Harry said the thing about getting the bench back, Pete said he'd talk to Eileen. That was when Floyd walked in and announced to the whole town that I was there. It sounded like Pete was going to talk to Eileen about when they would return the bench. Kim doesn't think she knows anything about it, but I'm seriously beginning to wonder. This morning Harry asked if I'd talked to Eileen. Why would he do that? Wouldn't he want to steer us away from the guilty parties? And he seemed genuinely upset on Friday when he came into the café yelling, 'Where in tarnation is my bench?'"

"Maybe he's just an incredibly good actor. Or maybe he wasn't in on it but he figured out who took it and they let him join their crime ring." Janet's laugh was more of a soft snort. "If the police captain didn't know that we are women of vast intellect and integrity, he'd think we were off our rockers if we told him our theory of organized crime in Dennison."

The picture that conjured in Debbie's mind was rather hilarious. "You have to believe us, Ian. Yes, we know one of them is in a wheelchair and one is almost deaf, but we have proof this gang is dangerous."

"What should we call them? Grumpy Old Men doesn't work if Eileen is one of the culprits."

"It's not politically correct to draw attention to their age." Debbie added a note of faux chastisement. "Maybe we should just call them the Dennison Bench Bandits."

"Perfect. We should also find out if Ray is in on this caper."

As Janet slowed for a stop sign, Debbie's phone buzzed. "It's Carly O'Sullivan."

"Hi, Debbie." Carly's voice, as usual, was cheery. "Sorry I couldn't return your call earlier. Grandma had back-to-back doctor appointments all day."

"Is she okay?" Maybe a dumb question to ask about a person in her nineties.

"'Fit as a fiddle.' Her words, not mine, but she's remarkably healthy. I was just thinking the other day how amazing it is that there are so many people from her generation still going strong. Must be something in the water."

"Let's hope so." It seemed like a good time to transition to the reason she'd left a message for Carly. And now she knew more than she had when she'd called. "Does she get together with any of the others? Eileen or Ray Zink or Pete Kimball or Harry Franklin?"

"Oh yes, on a regular basis. Grandma, Harriet Woodson, Floyd Marsh, Pete Kimball, Harry, Ray, and Eileen meet once a month.

Eileen is the ringleader. She calls them all together at Good Shepherd, and the staff cooks a special meal for them."

So there were actually seven members of the Bench Bandits. Maybe they should change the name to the Dennison Senior Seven. Carly had used the word *ringleader*. Was that just an expression, or did she know something? "Must be some interesting conversations when they all get together."

"I'm sure there are, but nobody under eighty-five is allowed in. It's all very secretive." Carly laughed. "I really believe that's what keeps Grandma going. She loves all of us, of course, but she has a comradery with her peers that she can't have with her family. They've supported each other through good times and bad for years. When my dad passed, Eileen and Harriet called Grandma every day for months, and the men stopped by regularly with flowers or doughnuts or just to sit and listen to her memories of her son. I dread the day they have to say goodbye to one of their own."

"What a beautiful bond. Especially when you think of how many elderly people are all alone."

"I know. Anyway, I'm sure you called for a reason. I didn't mean to go off on a tangent about our very senior citizens."

"Actually, that really wasn't a tangent." As an idea started forming, Debbie looked to Janet, hoping for approval for what she was about to say. "I was wondering if your grandmother might be up for a visit. Janet and I are going to start interviewing some of our longtime residents about their holiday memories, especially those involving the Christmas train and the bench."

Janet pulled up in front of the depot, turned the car off, and gave her a thumbs-up.

"I love that idea," Carly said. "I just left Good Shepherd. Grandma was napping, but I could meet you there in about an hour, if that works for you. I know she'd love to talk to you and show you her photo albums."

"Wonderful. We'll see you then." After saying goodbye, Debbie looked at Janet. "What have I gotten us into?"

"A gold mine. That's brilliant. It will give us lots of great stuff to tell the *Ohio Heritage* reporter, plus an excuse to talk to our suspects about the bench."

"Which might just flush out the culprit."

Debbie gave her a conspiratorial grin. "That's some slick sleuthing, my friend. Let the interviewing begin."

As they finished decorating the café, Debbie and Janet made notes for their Grinch party, taking turns scrolling on their phones for menu and table decoration ideas. The plans continued as they drove to the retirement home. Debbie read off the beginnings of a guest list. "Did I forget any potential Bench Bandits?"

"I can't think of any more. If everything goes well, we'll have all of our suspects in one place."

They parked in the Good Shepherd parking lot and walked up to the covered portico. Madeline and Carly met them just inside the door. Madeline O'Sullivan did not look ninety-three years old. Nor did she act it. She wore a knee-length flowered skirt and an emerald-green satin blouse that brought out the color of her eyes. On her feet were black ballet slippers, and her thick, silver-streaked hair was done in a sleek chignon, likely by Carly, who owned Serenity Salon & Spa on Main Street. Dangly green and silver earrings completed her ensemble. She held out her hand to Janet and then to Debbie. "I saw your mother at the clinic this morning, Debbie. You look so much like her."

"I've heard that a few times."

"You are both beautiful. Come in. We've got tea waiting in my apartment." Madeline, taller than her granddaughter by several inches and still walking with graceful, erect posture, rested one hand on Carly's shoulder and motioned for them to follow.

As they walked down a wide hallway lit by skylights and accented with hanging baskets of green vines, Debbie couldn't help but compare Madeline's demeanor to Rita Carson's. There was a night-and-day difference between the two. She remembered something her grandmother had once told her. "You don't get to be a sweet little old lady just by getting old." *Note to self: Start working on sweet now.*

"Cozy" was definitely the word to describe the nook surrounded by floor-to-ceiling bookshelves in Madeline's two-room apartment. Four plush swivel chairs upholstered in navy and off-white chevron print were clustered around a coffee table. On the table, a flowered china teapot and four matching cups sat on a copper tray beside a plate of colorful sugar cookies. A small glass jar of honey, slices of lemon, and a pitcher of cream took up the rest of the space on the tray. "This is lovely," Debbie said. It wasn't a word she used often, but nothing else fit.

Janet settled in one of the chairs. "We're usually the ones serving tea. This is nice for a change."

"Every woman deserves to be pampered once in a while." Madeline sat down and gave a slight nod to Carly. "My hands aren't quite as steady as they once were, or I would serve you myself." As Carly poured the tea, Madeline said, "My whole family is so sad about the bench going missing."

The statement seemed genuine. But she could have been telling the truth about her family's reaction and still have had something to do with its disappearance.

Madeline gestured toward a thick photo album decorated with hand-painted holly leaves and bright red berries. "We've had our family pictures taken there since 1944. I'll help in any way I can. I understand you're collecting Christmas memories."

Janet nodded, answered Carly's question about what she wanted in her tea, then started by telling them about the "Who Stole Christmas?" party. "We're thinking that sharing some warmhearted stories might draw attention to the importance of getting the bench returned. We're especially interested in memories surrounding the depot. The Christmas train, family photos taken on the bench, things like that. They don't necessarily have to be your own stories either. We'd love to hear some that have been passed down through generations."

"Well then, maybe I'll try to do this in chronological order."

Debbie thanked Carly for her cup of tea sweetened with honey then turned back to Madeline. "Would you mind if we record you?"

"Not at all. What are you going to do with the stories?"

"If we get enough, I may compile them in a booklet," Debbie said. "Wouldn't that make a great souvenir, especially for people who come to Dennison just to ride the train?"

Carly stopped in the midst of handing a cup to Madeline. "I love that idea. Can I preorder a dozen for the spa gift shop?"

Janet laughed. "I think you're onto something, Deb."

"So, stories…" Madeline blew on her tea, took a sip, and said, "The oldest story about the bench I know was told by my husband's grandfather, Collin O'Sullivan. Collin's grandfather, Camden O'Sullivan, whose parents came from Ireland in the 1840s, was a second-generation coal miner. There were seven children in the family, all of them boys. They were dirt-poor, but every morning as they held hands to pray over breakfast, Camden's father would say, 'Lord, we give Ye our boys to do with as Ye please. I'm only askin' that Ye make their lives a tad better than their da's.'

"Camden had a passion for two things, hunting and sketching. His father scoffed at his art, calling it a foolish waste of time, but when word got around that the Pittsburgh, Cincinnati and St. Louis Railway was going to locate the country's largest railroad shops and yards in the area and that the Dennison Land Company had bought up four hundred acres and planned to lay out a town along with the rail yards, Camden marched into one of their surveyors' tents and told them he could draw maps and shoot a bobcat from fifty yards with a bow and arrow, and that he knew the area like the back of his hand. He offered to be their guide, and they hired him on the spot.

"The next Christmas, Camden surprised his parents with a new house. He had it all decked out with pine boughs and a roaring fire when he brought them in. According to Grandpa Collin, Camden's father cried like a baby."

"And that house," Carly added, "still stands on my parents' land. My husband and I are fixing up the original log home to rent it out as a bed and breakfast."

"That's beautiful." Debbie checked the recorder to make sure it was still running.

"The Christmas part of that story doesn't end there," Madeline added. "Camden got jobs for all six of his brothers and his father at the rail yards. No O'Sullivan ever worked in a coal mine again. Camden went on to become a well-known cartographer, but he never forgot his beginnings. Every Christmas, he blessed a down-on-their-luck family with a new home. He did that up until he died at ninety-four."

For several moments, no one said a word. Then Janet said, "What an amazing man."

Debbie thought of a few things she'd heard about Madeline. She was a potter who had taught private ceramics classes for years and started a scholarship fund for art students. "From what I've heard, Camden's legacy of giving is still being carried on by your family."

Madeline smiled. "Which is why I want to help you find out what happened to the bench. I'd like to donate to the reward I heard you're offering. Do you think two thousand dollars will help motivate people to be looking? And to be honest?"

Dumbfounded, all Debbie could do was stare at Madeline, then Janet, and then nod in unison with her equally stunned best friend.

"Good. Now let's all have a cookie and enjoy some pictures, and I'll tell you more O'Sullivan Christmas tales."

December 12, 1942

Laverne Brenton tilted her head back and laughed at her boyfriend's joke. Margie joined in, hoping it didn't sound as strained as it felt. Jonathan Goldman was indeed funny. His easy humor, combined with the fact that he looked like a blond version of a young Clark Gable, made it hard for her to see him as any kind of threat. But tonight was her chance to search for clues.

Miraculously, last night at Andrea's party, she had garnered an invitation to dinner at Jonathan's apartment. Jonathan was the one who had extended the invitation...to her alone. Was it Margie's imagination, or had he flinched when Laverne included Andrea?

Now, in his apartment, Margie studied him, looking for any hint that he wasn't who he said he was. As he regaled them and four other guests with stories of his adventures with college buddies hiking in the Colorado mountains and deep-sea fishing off the coast of Maine, she caught a few words with just the slightest German accent. Or was it her imagination again? After three more stories, Margie turned to Laverne. "May I use your bathroom?" It was all part of the plan.

Andrea had a conversation starter planned to distract Jonathan while she was gone.

Laverne jumped up and led the way down the hall. "There you go." She bent close to Margie's ear. "I've tried to add a few feminine touches." She rested fingertips with bright red nails on a light blue hand towel edged in satin. "I keep teasing him that he lives like he doesn't plan on staying here. Look." She pulled on one side of the mirror above the sink, opening the medicine cabinet. She was right. Two of the three shelves were empty. The bottom shelf held a comb, a tube of Colgate Dental Cream, and one of Brylcreem.

"That's men for you. They don't like frills and fuss. I haven't seen any photographs on the walls." Margie kept her tone light and casual.

"He has a couple. I'll show you." Laverne led the way across the hall to a bedroom that was as stark as the bathroom. Nothing adorned the white walls. The bed was covered with a navy blue spread. A straight-backed chair took up one corner. The only other piece of furniture was a highboy. A wallet, a small pile of change, a few loose keys, and two picture frames on top of the dresser were the only things that kept Ravenna Park apartment 213 from looking like an unoccupied hotel room. Laverne pointed at one photo, and Margie glanced over her shoulder toward the door *before picking it up. "That's* my *Jonathan and his mother," Laverne said, emphasizing "my."*

The picture showed a woman in a low-waisted dress and cloche hat from the twenties, holding the hand of a little boy in shorts and suspenders. No, not shorts and suspenders. Lederhosen. *Margie had first seen them worn by waiters at a Bavarian restaurant in Cleveland. "So cute. Where did he grow up?"*

"In Milwaukee. This was taken at a German festival there."

Margie leaned in closer and studied the building in the background. Exposed timbers formed squares filled in with brick. She couldn't be sure, but it certainly looked like a thatched roof. She squinted. There were hills behind the building. High, rolling hills. "Hmm. My father's brother lives in Milwaukee." And I'm pretty sure that's not where your boyfriend grew up.

CHAPTER ELEVEN

*D*ebbie scooted her chair closer to Janet's then opened the front cover of the O'Sullivan Christmas photo album. On the first page, labeled *Christmas 1943*, was a black-and-white photograph of a man and woman with two young girls, one blond, one with long dark hair, sitting on the depot bench. A large bow and a sprig of greens festooned each end.

"That's me," Madeline said, pointing to the girl with the dark hair. "I was thirteen, and my sister, Sheila, was eleven. My mother worked at the furniture factory during the war, so our neighbor, Molly O'Sullivan, who had only boys, took us with her when she volunteered at the depot with the Salvation Army."

"I take it," Janet said, "that one of her boys liked the girl next door."

Madeline smiled. "Tommy O'Sullivan stole my heart when I was twelve and never gave it back. We were married for sixty-two wonderful years."

"That's beautiful."

"Molly was in charge of scheduling and planning for the food at the canteen. Whenever we weren't in school, Sheila and I were at the depot cutting homemade bread and making sandwiches. I don't think I'm exaggerating when I say I'd probably made five thousand sandwiches by the time I turned sixteen." She tapped on one of the bows. "The bench was brand-new. There were other benches, of course, one under a giant oak tree in front of the depot, but this one was so sturdy and the wood grain so pretty. It quickly became everyone's favorite place for photographs. It was Molly's idea to decorate it."

"Wow." Janet's single word expressed what Debbie felt. Though she'd seen dozens of similar pictures, this one had the feeling of stepping back in time. "Do you know who JB and MM were?"

"Margie McGarry and Jesse Blackwell. I think it was Margie's father that started the furniture factory. She was a volunteer at the depot. Jesse was in the army. He had that bench made with their initials already on it. Then, when he proposed, he teased her that she couldn't say no, because it would cause too much gossip. She said yes, and they got married at Faith Community Church. It was such a beautiful ceremony." Madeline smiled, and Debbie felt she was seeing the young romance through the eyes of a starry-eyed teen.

"The first time I saw them together, a year before he proposed to her, I could tell something was wrong. He had just gotten off the train, and she went running to him, but instead of hugging her, he practically pushed her away from him, and it looked like they were arguing. When the train left, I saw her read a note. I thought she was going to cry, but she went back to work. I asked Molly about it, and she told me to mind my own business. I was off to college by the time all the rumors about them started. I wish I'd been more interested. All I know for sure is that Margie and Jesse were spies."

A surge of adrenaline shot through Debbie. "Spies...for the US?"

"Yes. They did something to help the war effort, but no one knew about it at the time." Madeline sighed. "I wish my mother-in-law was still around. She had so many stories to tell about those days."

Debbie turned another page in the album, buying time to process. Not only did they have a lead on a wartime romance involving the bench, now they had to chase down the rest of a story involving espionage. She paged through family photos taken in front of Christmas trees and snowmen. Smiling babies and stockings and a puppy in a box. And then a group shot, black-and-white and slightly blurred by falling snow, grabbed her attention. Three women sat on the bench. Two men crouched on the left side, and one on the other. A young man in a Pullman uniform stood a foot from the bench, hands on a luggage cart. Though he was in profile, it was clear he wore a broad grin.

"That was taken in February, 1943," Madeline said. "Recognize anyone?"

Debbie tapped on the photo. "I recognize Eileen. We have a lot of photos of her from the forties. And"—she pointed at the man facing the opposite direction—"is that Harry? Did he get in the picture by accident?"

"That was Harry. And that was no accident."

"Who are the others?"

Madeline smiled and shook her head as if recalling a happy memory. "You couldn't have assembled a more incongruent bunch of friends if you tried. Floyd Marsh, Pete Kimball, Ray Zink, Harriet Woodson, Eileen, and"—she pointed at the woman in the middle—"Margie."

Debbie stared at Margie. The woman the bench had been made for. And, if Madeline's story was correct, Dennison's own homegrown spy.

"Why aren't you in the picture?" Janet asked.

"I *took* the picture. Harry and I were just kids. We became friends with them years later. All but Margie. She'd moved away by then." She pointed to Harry. "They all loved Harry. They wanted him in the picture, but he refused. Had he been caught fooling around on the job, he could have been fired. So he made it look unintentional."

Debbie thought of the man who'd stormed into the café on Friday morning. "He was a very smart man, even then."

"This town, and the railroad, owe him a debt of gratitude. He always acted with respect, but he pushed envelopes that needed to be ripped wide open. Even though Black soldiers were discriminated against in the service when it came to pay, promotions, and medical care and were segregated into their own regiments commanded by white officers, here in our depot they were treated equally because of Harry opening our eyes. Molly and Eileen wouldn't tolerate anything less. There was one time—" Madeline gave her knee a soft slap. "Let's go talk to Eileen. She's got more stories than I have. Or have you already interviewed her?"

"No, we haven't." Eileen's room was just down the hall, and they now had the perfect reason to talk to her. Maybe, while asking for stories, they'd learn something Kim hadn't. "That's a great idea."

Madeline gripped the arms of her chair, and Carly stood and deftly wedged her foot underneath it to keep it from turning while she helped steady her as Margie eased to a stand.

As they walked slowly down the well-lit hallway, Debbie made a mental list of things to bring up to hopefully find out what, if anything, Eileen knew about the bench. Was she, indeed, one of the Bench Bandits? The thought made her smile. How, exactly, would a group of people pushing a hundred pull off a heist? And what would be their motive? Had they somehow heard of a plot devised by one of the *Ohio Heritage* competitors and hidden it away for safekeeping? Or did they not want all the publicity that winning the contest could bring? That hypothesis didn't jive with what Floyd had said about a mystery being good for the town. Any way she tried to picture the seven of them meeting to devise a plan just didn't make sense.

Each room had a name plaque and a small shelf next to the door. A clear glass nativity scene on a piece of midnight-blue velvet sat on Eileen's shelf. Behind it was a sign that read WISE MEN STILL SEEK HIM. Madeline knocked then poked her head in. "Eileen? It's Madeline. I've got some company with me. Are you decent?"

"I am," came the cheerful answer. "Come on in."

The white-walled room was decorated in aqua and beige with touches of peach. A large picture window looked out on a pond surrounded by mature trees, a scene that would be stunning in any season. Eileen sat in a tan recliner in one corner, her feet elevated, pillows behind her back, and a snowy white throw with sparkly threads woven throughout covering her legs. A small white Christmas tree with teal lights sat on the table beside her, casting a cool glow about the room.

Madeline started to introduce them, but Eileen waved away her words with the same gesture that told them to sit down, Janet and Madeline on a love seat and Debbie in a folding chair she pulled from between the end of the bed and the wall. "How are things at the café, girls?"

"Getting busier by the day," Janet answered.

"I suppose people are upset about the bench not being there. What's being done to find it?" As if trying to appear taller than her something-less-than five feet, Eileen scooted back in the recliner that made her appear even smaller than she was.

Debbie studied her, watching for any hint of "I know something you don't" but didn't get any clues from the serious expression on Eileen's lined face.

"The police are looking, and"—Debbie glanced at Madeline with a smile—"there will be a reward offered to anyone who provides information that leads to its return." She leaned forward. "Do you have any idea what might have happened to it?"

"What would someone do with a big old bench? If a person took it, they couldn't leave it out where anyone could see it. What do you think?"

"We have a few theories but nothing solid," Debbie said. "We're having trouble figuring out what someone's motive might be. Do you have any ideas?"

"Hmm." Eileen rested a beautifully manicured but clearly arthritic finger on her chin. "I read a lot of mysteries. People are mostly motivated by greed, envy, love, and bitterness. And then I suppose there are times when we do things that appear bad because we're trying to protect someone. Think of Rahab in the Bible who lied to protect the spies or Sarah who lied to protect Abraham. I was just listening to an audiobook about a Quaker woman who hid runaway slaves in her barn. She saved the lives of more than twenty people by breaking the law. So I suppose the answer to your question is, I don't know."

They were getting nowhere. Janet's expression said she felt the same, but she copied Debbie's posture, leaning closer to Eileen, and said, "We're also looking for nostalgic Christmas stories, especially ones surrounding the depot."

"Goodness. I could keep you here for days."

"Would you mind if we record you?"

"Not at all. What are you going to do with the stories?"

"I'm thinking about compiling them into a booklet to sell to visitors," Debbie said.

Eileen pressed her hands together. "What a wonderful idea. I can't wait to buy one. At my age, I'm looking for any way to pass on a century's worth of adventures to future generations." She gestured to a box sitting on the end of her bed. "I was actually just going through some old ornaments. Go ahead and open it."

Janet was sitting closest, so she put the box on her lap and lifted the lid. The inside was divided by cardboard partitions into sixteen individual compartments, each containing an ornament and a piece of paper. "I love old ornaments," she said. "We've decided to use only vintage Christmas decorations at the café."

"Pick one," Eileen instructed.

Janet picked up what looked like a real egg with an oval cut out of one side. It was painted dark blue with a white star on top. Inside was a tiny manger with a baby. Debbie unfolded the paper left in the compartment. She glanced at Eileen, who nodded, and began to read. "'Christmas 1942. Linda March, Margie McGarry, Esther Davis, Madeline and Sheila Doyle, and I made these for the Christmas tree at the depot. We brushed them with glue first to make them strong, then paint, and then shellac. First we made two dozen of them. Then some of the men who were heading home wanted to buy them, so we ended up giving them away and then made many more.'"

"That was just before I took over as stationmaster," Eileen said. "I was a volunteer at the time, and we were trying to give the depot a homey touch. One of the girls who was raised on a farm taught us how to make them, and the first day they were on the tree, men started offering us money for them because they hadn't had a chance to shop for wives or moms or girlfriends. So we started spending evenings making them. We had a regular assembly line with stations for painting and making little figures out of clay, and we'd rotate every half hour. The worst job was blowing out the eggs."

Eileen rubbed a finger under her ear. "We'd put a small pin hole at the top and a slightly larger one at the bottom and then blow on the top, and the whole egg would come out of the bottom, yolk still intact." She laughed. "We ate so many eggs. I suppose today there would be health codes forbidding eating eggs that were blown out like that, but during the war we couldn't waste anything." She held out her hand, and Janet carefully set the delicate egg on her palm. "We each kept one. I gave this one to my mother." She looked up at Madeline. "Do you still have yours?"

Madeline shook her head. "I saw Harry admiring the one I was going to keep. I'd put a tiny clay snowman in it, and he said his mother would love it. I knew he couldn't afford to buy her anything, so I gave it to him."

"I suppose Margie saved hers for Jesse," Madeline prompted.

"Actually, if memory serves, she was going to a Christmas party and she needed a homemade gift." Eileen laughed. "Strange that I can remember that, but don't ask me what pajamas I wore to bed last night."

"I remember Molly complaining that Margie was never around on weekends," Madeline said. "Where did she go?"

Eileen nodded. "I remember that. I don't know if she ever told anyone where she was going. She went to Kent State until the war started. I'm guessing she had friends up there."

"Wasn't that kind of extravagant with gas rationing?" Janet asked.

Madeline's eyes lit. "I haven't thought about it in decades, but that was something else Molly wasn't happy with. I overheard her grumbling to someone that it wasn't fair that she didn't have gas to go visit her own mother in Akron more than once a month but Margie McGarry flitted around on Uncle Sam's dollar when that gas should be used to bring our soldiers back home safe. I remember thinking that if we lost the war, Molly was going to blame it all on Margie." She tipped her head as she addressed Eileen. "I suppose that had something to do with her espionage work. Was she actually working for the government?"

"I don't know. She and Jesse got some kind of award for something, but that was years after the war, and they weren't living here. I was busy raising a family and didn't pay much attention. Anyway, these ladies want some feel-good stories. We've got fifteen more ornaments to look at." Eileen laughed and handed the egg back to Janet. She pointed to an ornament that appeared to be a child's toy train engine with a small gold loop glued to the top. "Let me tell you about the Great Snowstorm of 1944. It was December tenth, and…"

For the next hour, Eileen regaled them with Christmas stories. When she appeared to be tiring, Janet said they'd return soon for more.

"You'd better. We've still got half a dozen ornaments to talk about. I tell you what, take them. We'll talk about them some other time, but they're too big for my tree, and Kim has the ones that have meaning to her personally. Each of these tells a bit of Dennison history. They belong at the depot. And I surely won't be needing them where I'm eventually going." Her eyes shimmered with what seemed to Debbie to be expectation. She wondered if she would possess that kind of "looking forward" attitude if she lived as long as Eileen had.

They were saying their goodbyes when a male voice Debbie recognized shouted Eileen's name from the hallway. "Eileen," he repeated, "put everything away, quick! I just heard the two—Oh." Ray Zink rolled into view in his wheelchair. "Didn't know you had company." His weathered face was flushed. "Sorry to interrupt." He started backing up.

Debbie waved. "Stay. We're getting ready to—" But he'd already reached the hallway.

"What was that all about?" Janet asked.

"Probably nothing."

The two words, said in perfect unison by Madeline and Eileen, convinced Debbie it was definitely not nothing.

CHAPTER TWELVE

ebbie walked into the café early on Tuesday morning carrying two boxes. The small one on top contained the "Who Stole Christmas?" party flyers she'd stayed up late designing and printing. The larger box held the ornaments Eileen had given them.

A rich caramel aroma greeted her when she walked into the kitchen, but something was different. It reminded her of breakfast with her cousins at her grandma's house when she was young. Janet had her back to her, pulling something out of the oven. "Pancakes?"

"Nope." Wearing oven mitts, and with the utmost concentration on her face, Janet put a rectangular tray on top of a pan of cinnamon rolls then flipped the pan over. Biting her bottom lip, she lifted the glass pan.

Debbie stepped closer, and a groan escaped her lips as thick, gooey, hot caramel cascaded down the sides of the giant rolls studded with pecans.

Janet exhaled. "I used maple syrup in place of most of the brown sugar. I was afraid they'd stick. That would have been a nightmare, since I've got three more pans in the oven."

"I'm pretty sure heaven's going to smell just like this." Debbie took a deep breath and reached for two small plates. "If this is a new recipe, it has to go through quality control before we can serve it."

Janet complied with a smile, plating one and handing Debbie a serrated knife. "We really should let it cool first."

"No time. Or patience." With a gentle sawing motion, Debbie sliced through the sticky top and into the hot, fluffy center then slid half onto another plate.

Janet pulled the rest of the maple pecan rolls from the oven. Each batch slid easily from its pan, and the two friends stood for a moment, simply admiring the glistening amber-colored masterpieces. "Hope they're a hit."

Debbie laughed. "If I were a betting woman, I'd put money on them all being gone by nine o'clock." She picked up her roll and blew on it then took a careful bite and closed her eyes. After chewing slowly and swallowing, she said, "And I'm hoping that's what heaven tastes like."

"Speaking of heaven," Janet said, "don't you love Eileen's view on life? I get the feeling that even though she still expects to have a lot more good times in this world, she can't wait for the adventures to begin in the next."

"Let's start making it a habit to talk, and think, like that. Maybe we can find a retro 'This is the first day of the rest of your life' sign."

"I like that."

Debbie looked across the kitchen to the window where the sun was just beginning to make its presence known with slim fingers of gold. And then headlights slashed across the scene. "Kim's here. Let's tell her about what Ray said. We're in agreement that we were probably the 'two' he was talking about, right?"

Janet sank a fork into her half of the cinnamon roll and held it up, examining it from all sides. "Yep. What could he have been telling her to put away?"

"Maybe they've started a gambling ring and he was warning her to put the poker chips away." Debbie laughed. It was just too hard to imagine any of them involved in something shady.

"Or maybe they aren't only the Bench Bandits. Maybe they've been filching other things to finance that bucket list adventure Kim talked about."

Debbie pointed to the first pan Janet had taken out. "If there are any of these left at the end of the day, let's take them to Good Shepherd. You know your baking makes people talk."

"It's my secret truth-serum cinnamon."

Debbie finished her last bite, licked her fingers, and then walked around the counter and washed her hands. When she finished drying them, Janet held out a plated roll and a fork. "Take this to Kim. See if she can make any sense out of what Ray said."

"Will do." Debbie took the plate.

Kim was just turning on the display case lights when Debbie walked into the museum. "Good morning!" she greeted. "It's a cold one, but we're supposed to have full sun all day."

"That will help." Debbie tapped the fork against the plate. "I brought you something."

"Oh my. I can feel my pants getting tighter just looking at that." She took a bite, closed her eyes, and groaned exactly the way Debbie had. After she swallowed, she said, "Tell Janet she better be prepared to sell out before noon."

"I already did."

"I heard you two had a visit with Mom and Madeline yesterday."

"We did. And speaking of us two…" She told her about Ray's awkward visit.

"Hmm. That's confirmation that it's not all my imagination. You know, one day last week I stopped in to see Mom without telling her I was coming. When I walked in, she was stuffing something in the drawer of her bedside table. She practically slammed the drawer then tried to act like nothing was out of the ordinary. I assumed she had candy stashed in there. She's supposed to be watching her sugar intake, but she does love her sour gumdrops."

"Janet and I think they're operating a gambling racket or a jewel theft ring."

Kim laughed. "Well, I might feel better about one of those than the thought of them renting Harleys for a cross-country trip. Hopefully they'd be able to serve out their life sentences right there at Good Shepherd." She shook her head. "Sorry. My sense of humor gets a little wacky sometimes."

"Laughter is good medicine. I think you got that gift from your mom. A wacky sense of humor just might be one of the keys to longevity." She waved as she started for the door. "Let me know if you find out what she's hiding."

"You'll be the first to hear. Right after I report the Good Shepherd crime ring to the authorities."

As Debbie walked back to the café, she spotted Crosby trotting ahead of Harry. She turned over the Open sign and held the door for them. Crosby walked in first, his master right behind him. "Any word on the bench?" Harry asked, by way of greeting.

"Nothing yet." Knowing that the eyes are the windows to the soul, she tried to get a good look at his face, but his slightly stooped posture, likely from years of toting baggage for customers who didn't all treat him like Jackie Gleason had, made it difficult. Was he asking because he truly wanted to know, or because he was trying to find out if she was any closer to discovering the Bandits' crime? "Have you heard anything?"

He didn't answer until after he'd eased into his seat. "Just a lot of speculating."

"Any more thoughts about Michael Morgan?"

Harry shrugged. "Guess I took this a bit too personal at first, thinking about who would do that to *me*. But I still wouldn't put it past him. Some years back, when he and Patricia were still together, Michael helped me refinish that bench. We gave it a light sanding, careful not to mess with any of the names and dates, and then gave it a coat of triple-thick polyurethane. While we worked, we talked. I told him all of my memories about the bench, starting with the day it arrived. Good memories and bad. I remembered a woman during the war fainting when her man didn't get off the train and she found out he wasn't ever coming home. Swooned right onto that bench. Couples, like yourself, getting engaged on it. Even admitted that I kissed a girl for the first time right there." Harry gestured to the place where the bench should have been. "Anyway, by the time we finished, he knew how much it meant to me. If anyone ever wanted to hurt me, wrecking that bench would be like a dagger to my heart."

"I know Michael and Patricia had their problems, but do you really think he'd have motive to hurt you?"

Harry looked out the window. "Yes, I do. Don't tell her, but I ran into Michael about a month ago. He told me he'd changed and wanted to reconcile with Patricia. I told him if I ever caught him anywhere near her, I'd fix his clock. Not that I'm anyone to fear these days, but he knew I'd make his life miserable one way or another."

"You don't believe he's changed?"

Harry shrugged. "I guess I believe he believes he has, but we've all heard that before. I can't sit back and see my granddaughter get hurt again." He pointed across the table. "Patricia will be joining me."

So that was the end of the discussion. "I'll get your coffees."

"Do I smell pancakes?" Harry sniffed the air.

Debbie smiled. "That's exactly what I asked when I walked in this morning. Janet made maple pecan caramel rolls."

"Mm-mm. We'll each have one. Probably stick to my dentures, but what's that to grumble about at my age, right?"

"You're an inspiration, Harry. I think that's the second time in a few days I've said that."

"Keep it coming. Compliments are few and far between when you're almost a hundred."

She patted his shoulder, turned, and then pivoted back to face him. "I saw Eileen yesterday. I told her we wanted to record some of her Christmas memories for younger generations. I want to include you too. Maybe we could call it *Dennison's Greatest Generation's Christmas Memories*."

"Huh." Harry's face crinkled in a smile. "I like that. Guess we've accumulated a ton of Christmas experiences between us. And I'm sure we can give you a lot of variety."

"You know what I love about you and Eileen and Ray and Madeline and Floyd and the rest of your buddies? You still seem to be excited about life, like there's always something fun waiting around the corner. What's your latest adventure, Harry?"

This time she could see his face. Every smile line splaying out from his deep brown eyes. Every twitch of his bushy brows. "Oh, we're cookin' up something I can't talk about just yet." He looked over her shoulder and waved. Debbie turned and smiled at Patricia.

"What smells so heavenly?" Patricia asked.

Debbie described the cinnamon rolls. "I think we're going to rename them *Heavenly* Maple Pecan Caramel Rolls. Your grandpa has already ordered two."

"Can I get one to go also? There's a judge I'll be facing whose attitude could use a little sweetening."

"Smart lady."

"Any news on the bench?" Patricia asked.

"Nothing yet. Have you heard anything?" It crossed Debbie's mind that she should have an apron embroidered with those words. *Haven't heard anything about the bench yet. Have you?*

The rest of the day passed quickly. If she actually had been a betting woman, Janet would have had to pay up. The caramel rolls were all gone by nine, and by two o'clock, when they locked the door, Janet's second batch of four pans had also disappeared. When the kitchen and café were clean, they added Eileen's ornaments to their tree. Debbie was just reaching for her coat when there was a knock at the door. She turned to see Greg standing on the other side of the glass.

"Do you two have a date?" Janet whispered.

"We do not date," she whispered back before unlocking the door. "Hi!"

"Hi. I just thought of something. Remember a couple of months ago when somebody vandalized the mural over there?"

"Yes." She did remember. She'd gotten to work one morning in October and was saddened and angered to see that someone had sprayed graffiti on the painting of an old steam engine that took up the whole side of the real estate building across the street.

"The village installed a security camera after that incident." Greg strode to the front window and pointed. "On that utility pole."

"So…" Debbie studied the angle of the camera, and a jolt of adrenaline shot down her arms. "The bench might be on the video?"

Greg nodded, still staring out the window. He practically vibrated with excitement. "There hasn't been any more graffiti, so I don't know if anyone has ever had a reason to look at the feed." He turned toward her, his expression so much like one of Julian's she almost laughed. "Are you free?"

"Yes, she is." Janet grabbed Debbie's coat and draped it over her shoulders. "I'll lock up."

Giving her best friend a look that was supposed to appear stern, Debbie thanked her and walked out with Greg. "I take it we're going to go check out the security camera footage?"

"Yep. It's at the chamber office. I asked Regina to try to cue it up to Thursday night."

She asked about the boys and how Julian's report was coming along, and before she knew it they were walking in the door at the chamber of commerce building.

"All set." Regina, a high school senior who got out of school early three days a week to work at the chamber office, smiled up at Greg. Though she was way too young, she likely joined a dozen other females in town who had a crush on him. "Hi, Debbie." The greeting was almost an afterthought. "I went back to Thursday, right before dark." She stood and offered her chair to Debbie.

"Thanks, Regina. Good work." Greg smiled back at her, and the girl practically glowed. He pulled another chair close to Debbie, and they stared at the screen together. There was the bench, surrounded by a puddle of light from the streetlamp. He fast-forwarded until they saw a light-colored vehicle pull up in front of the depot and park in the No Parking zone, blocking their view of the bench. Greg rewound then pushed pause at 4:23 a.m.

An old, probably 1950s, pickup truck. Though the footage was in black-and-white, it took no stretch of the imagination to picture it as light green. The driver's side door opened. A figure got out. Like in hundreds of crime dramas Debbie had seen on TV, he wore a dark hoodie and kept his face hidden. He opened the tailgate, took out the old gas can and set it on the road, and then looked around while still keeping his head down, shielded by the hood. Then he took out something...

"A gun!" Debbie gasped.

Greg zoomed in then let out a loud breath. "A cordless drill."

Debbie's shoulders dropped on a sigh as she watched the figure walk around the truck, hidden from view.

A few minutes later, he reappeared, holding up one end of the bench. The other end was hefted by another person wearing a ball cap low on his forehead. The two were animated, shaking their heads. Though Debbie couldn't see faces, there was something about their movements that made her think they were laughing. The first person lifted his end onto the truck bed then shifted his position to help with the other end. As they lifted together, the passenger's cap blew off. "Recognize him?" Greg asked.

Debbie leaned closer, squinting at the screen. And then she saw something. Something too familiar. A long braid tumbling down the middle of the person's back. Her heart sank. "I think I recognize *her*."

CHAPTER THIRTEEN

ebbie finally found time on Tuesday night to decorate her Christmas tree. Though Janet had offered again to help, she was in desperate need of some alone time. She started a fire in the fireplace, found a collection of Christmas music from the 1940s and '50s on her phone, and heated a cup of milk in the microwave, letting Frank Sinatra's butter-smooth voice flow over her as she dumped a packet of hot chocolate into the milk. It was the kind with mini marshmallows, and she watched them bounce as she stirred. It had been a roller-coaster few days, and she felt a bit like the little blobs bobbing in her mug.

What was she to do with what she'd learned this afternoon? Greg had asked her if she was 100 percent sure it was Ashling Kelly she'd recognized on the security footage before he called the police. Oh, how she'd wanted to say no, but she was sure.

The surveillance tape showed her and the other person putting the bench in the pickup truck just before four thirty Friday morning. It was more than an hour later when Debbie had awakened to sirens. And Ian had said Ashling was in her own truck, a red Silverado, at the time of the accident. None of this made sense.

As she prayed for Ashling, questions swirled in her mind. What would this do to Colleen? To Ashling's business? To Tiffany and her other friends and the community in general?

The questions kept coming, repeating at regular intervals, invading the peace and quiet she'd been craving. Why would Ashling have taken the bench? Was it just a silly teenage prank? Who was the man she'd been helping? Greg had run the video backward and forward, but they hadn't been able to make out a license plate number. Would the police be able to enhance the recording and discover more?

With a sigh, she walked back to the living room. There was nothing she could do about it now.

She'd just set her mug on an end table when her phone dinged with an email. She smiled at the name. She hadn't talked to Stephanie, her college roommate, in almost two weeks. Strange that she'd email instead of calling. The subject line read, "Reminder!"

The party! Had she responded? Yes. With a "maybe," wondering if she dared ask Paulette to cover her at the café on a crazy-busy Dennison Christmas weekend just so she could attend a party of her old friends. But now…

As she read through the list of people invited to a Christmas party at Stephanie's place in Cleveland on Saturday afternoon, she felt a pinch of longing. They'd all first met at a women's business group meetings. Out of that grew an informal singles group. Over the years, as one by one almost everyone had gotten married, they'd simply called themselves "The Group."

She missed her old friends. She'd been in Cleveland several times since moving back to Dennison. Every time she visited, she'd been welcomed with open arms. And every time, the transition afterward to small-town life took a couple of days. She loved it here, but life moved at a much slower pace and, though she didn't miss the stress, sometimes she missed the hustle and bustle of the city. Coffee shops on every corner, plays and musicals and sporting events, always someone to do something with. And food. Oh, how she missed trying a different restaurant every weekend. Depending on her mood, she could choose Thai, Italian, Asian, Indian, or Mexican. Steak, seafood… And the bakeries. Fresh focaccia, scones, crusty herb breads, cassata cakes, pignoli cookies… Her stomach growled, even though she'd just finished a healthy salad chock-full of chicken and veggies.

Saturday the ninth. She'd be in Cleveland picking up Betsy anyway. Paulette had already agreed to work on Saturday. And maybe Betsy would appreciate a little time alone with her memories. A break from their walk through time would probably be a welcome respite after twenty-four hours of nonstop reminiscing. Debbie could stay at the party for a couple of hours and still be available for dinner with the woman who had almost become her mother-in-law.

She read through the party details. All the old traditions she'd been a part of for years. Ugly Christmas sweater. White elephant gift. Cookie exchange. Vote for your favorite Christmas movie. She'd missed this. It would be good to be home again. No… She edited her thought. *Dennison* was home. But it would be good to visit Cleveland again.

She was standing on a stool, attaching the star to the top of her tree, when her phone rang. Why was Pastor Nick calling on a Tuesday evening? She glanced at the clock. The elders met on Tuesday nights. They should be in the middle of a meeting right now. "Hello?"

"Hi, Debbie. It's Pastor Nick. I'm calling with an urgent need, but you know what I always say, right?"

She climbed down the stepladder. "'No is a perfectly acceptable answer.'"

"Yes. But I'd appreciate it if you'd hear me out and pray before you say no."

"Of course." Her stomach tightened. What committee did he want her to serve on? Or maybe, like once before, he was just calling to order doughnuts for a board meeting.

"Rick and Sara Overton's niece lives in Louisiana. She lost her husband and their business in the flooding after the hurricane last month, and she and her teenage daughter were planning to move in with Rick and Sara while their house was being rebuilt, but Rick just found out his cancer is back."

"I'm so sorry to hear that."

"We'll be organizing meals and doing whatever we can to help, but Sara's going to have her hands full taking care of Rick. The mom and daughter are already on their way up here and we—"

"Need a place for them to stay." As Debbie finished his sentence, she looked at the floor. She had two small guest rooms in the basement, and Betsy would be staying in one of them next week. She sat down on the couch then got up, turned around, and stared at the piece of furniture she'd just been sitting on. A queen-size hide-a-bed. She could give her Louisiana guests the basement, let Betsy have her room, and she could sleep in the living room for a few nights. *Lord, should I say yes?*

A sense of rightness in her spirit gave her confirmation. "They can certainly stay here. I'm leaving on Friday afternoon for the weekend, so they can have the place to themselves for a couple of days."

"You're sure?"

"Yes. Definitely."

"Wonderful. Hopefully, it will only be for a few days. We're working on finding an apartment for them. I'll call you in the morning with details."

She hung up, plopped back onto the couch, picked up her hot chocolate, and stared at the glow of hundreds of tiny white lights. This call, this interruption and inconvenience, had the feel of something ordained by God. As she leaned back, her toe struck something under the coffee table. The Box. She hadn't opened it in days. She'd planned to take time this month, like she did every year in the weeks leading up to the anniversary of her engagement, Reed's death, and the day that should have been her wedding day, to immerse herself in memories of the past. Instead, God was bringing a woman and child into her life whose grief was fresh and raw.

A call to live in the present.

Father, show me how to help them. Let me be gracious and kind and real with them. Let me be sensitive to their needs. If there's anything You've taught me that will help them, please bring it to mind at the right time. She took a sip from her mug. As warmth began to spread through her, she knew it was not just from the hot chocolate. It was more than that. It was a sense of purpose. A Bible verse she'd memorized years ago came to mind. *Praise be to the God and Father of our Lord Jesus Christ, the Father of compassion and the God of all comfort, who comforts us in all our troubles, so that we can comfort those in any trouble with the comfort we ourselves receive from God.*

As she closed her eyes, savoring the warmth, Bing Crosby began to croon, "I'm dreaming tonight..." She smiled as the chorus began. "I'll be home for Christmas..."

Debbie was once again awake long before the sun. By six, she'd dusted the guest rooms and put fresh sheets on the beds. She stood in the doorway of one of the basement rooms and remembered how it had looked when she moved in. Just a wide-open room with a cement floor and walls. But she'd been impressed by the height of the ceilings, unusual in a place this old. That had stirred her imagination and, thankfully, Greg—the contractor she'd hired to do all of her remodeling—had caught her vision. And maybe a bit of her heart in the process.

Shaking her head to keep her thoughts on task, she admired the furnishings. An estate sale had provided antique mission-style beds and dressers, and she'd found two old quilts in great shape at a resale store. With the crown molding Greg had used to trim each room, they looked like they could have been here all along. She stepped out into the small but cozy sitting room and prayed it would be a serene place for her guests to rest and recover.

Upstairs, she cleared off the top of her dresser, a place that always collected earrings, loose change, and anything she found in her pockets before doing laundry. She would put fresh sheets on her bed before leaving on Friday morning so it would be ready for Betsy.

When the bedrooms were in order, she took chicken out of the fridge and put it in the slow cooker. They'd have creamed chicken and biscuits for dinner. With a fresh salad and something warm and sweet, maybe apple crisp with ice cream for dessert, she'd welcome her guests with comfort food.

As she peeled and chopped carrots and celery, she wondered if tonight would be awkward. She'd been to New Orleans several times, but that was the extent of her experience in Louisiana. She remembered one adorable server at a seafood restaurant she and Stephanie had gone to for a fish boil who'd called them Miss Debbie and Miss Stephanie and taught them how to eat crawfish. "Jus' pinch the tail and suck the heads." They'd had to listen closely over the din of the restaurant, trying to decipher the rest of her instructions in a slow Southern drawl peppered with creole. Would there be a language barrier between her and her guests? She imagined it went both ways, with her Midwest accent being as hard for them to figure out. This was one of those situations her mother would label MGR…much grace required.

On Thursday morning, December 7, before Kim arrived, Debbie stood alone in the depot lobby in front of an exhibit labeled A Day of Infamy.

Eighty-two years ago on this date, life in Dennison was normal. The lobby may have been filled with people taking a Sunday trip to visit family or shop in a larger city. Laughter and happy chatter had probably ricocheted off the high ceiling as people waited with anticipation to board the train for a day of fun.

Few people in Dennison were thinking much about war. But that was all about to change.

She studied the timeline.

Sunday, December 7

3:42 a.m.

An officer on the the USS Condor *spots a periscope at the entrance of Pearl Harbor. This information is relayed by the* Condor *to a destroyer, the USS* Ward.

6:00 a.m.

Using a Honolulu radio station's music as a guide, the Japanese come in for their first attack wave from the air.

6:45 a.m.

Lt. William Outerbridge gives the command to open fire. The second volley from the destroyer sinks the submarine.

7:55 a.m.

Japanese dive-bombers target airfields and Battleship Row, sinking the USS West Virginia *and USS* Oklahoma. *USS* Arizona *suffers heavy losses, then the forward ammunition magazine of the ship ignites after a second horizontal attack. Blazing furiously, the* Arizona *sinks. Four other ships suffer damage.*

8:54 a.m.

Another wave of Japanese aircraft attack the USS Pennsylvania *and bomb three destroyers as well as the USS* Nevada.

10:00 a.m.

Japanese planes begin hitting gasoline tankers.

Debbie dropped her gaze to the summary at the bottom.

America's losses were catastrophic and included 2,403 casualties, including civilians. Another 1,000 were wounded. The Japanese lost 129 soldiers.

On December 8 President Roosevelt gave his famous "Infamy" speech to Congress, and the United States formally declared war on Japan.

Looking around the depot, Debbie imagined overhead speakers playing music, adding to the festive feeling of Christmas travelers. And then, midafternoon, the music stops. An announcer breaks in. "The Japanese have bombed Pearl Harbor!"

What would that feel like? As long as she lived, she would never forget the morning of September 11, 2001, standing in a crowd in the student union, staring in disbelief as a plane flew into the second of the twin towers. It didn't take much to relive the fear.

Moving over a couple of feet, she stood in front of a portrait of Eleanor Roosevelt above the words she spoke to the nation on the evening of the 1941 attack. Debbie skimmed until words near the bottom caught her attention.

We must go about our daily business more determined than ever to do the ordinary things as well as we can and when we find a way to do anything more in our communities to help others, to build morale, to give a feeling of security, we must do it.

Unexpectedly, Debbie felt her eyes burn. It didn't take much to imagine the emotions coursing through the people huddled around radios all across the country. She'd lived it. Maybe on a smaller scale, but she could remember the days following 9/11 as if it were yesterday. Quietly, she repeated the words, "'We must go about our daily business more determined than ever to do the ordinary things as well as we can.'"

Didn't that still apply?

December 13, 1942

As she walked out of church with Andrea, Margie wrapped her tweed coat snugly around herself and cinched the belt. The heavy sky threatened snow, though Ravenna hadn't seen any yet this year.

Andrea donned her dusty-rose beret as they walked down the steps. "Timely message today," she said, winking at Margie.

"Guess you could call it timely. It made me squirm a bit." Andrea's pastor was preaching a series on the Ten Commandments. Today he'd focused on the ninth, Exodus 20:16, "Thou shalt not bear false witness against thy neighbour." In light of her deception, his words had made her uncomfortable.

"Why?" Andrea tipped her head to stare at her. "We're not bearing false witness. We're uncovering the

truth about someone who is. He's pretending to be someone he's not. And who knows how many other commandments he has broken or plans to. He's stolen, for sure, and he's probably devising a plan to break the sixth one."

Margie stopped walking, her pulse pounding in her ears. "Murder?"

"Well, it's possible, isn't it?"

"Jesse's message specifically mentioned Christmas Eve, didn't it? The plant will be shut down, so he can sneak in and get more files. If he wanted to do something...worse...wouldn't he plan it for when he could inflict the most"—Margie swallowed hard—"damage?"

"Maybe." Andrea started walking again. "Or maybe he's gotten all the information he needs to make der Führer *happy*, and now he's going to make sure we never produce another weapon. And even though the plant is closed, there will still be guards on duty."

Margie's mouth went dry. What had she agreed to? She'd known this mission of theirs involved secrets that, in the hands of the enemy, could be used against the US. She'd known it could be dangerous. But murder? And destruction on the scale Andrea was suggesting? "I g-guess I've been naive. This is...bigger than I thought."

"Which makes it even more crucial that we uncover the truth. Quickly."

"But shouldn't your father, or someone in the military, take this on? If there are guards, shouldn't they be informed to be on the lookout?"

"Yes." Andrea nodded so vigorously her beret fell off. "In a perfect world. But Jonathan has my father completely deceived. You heard him last night."

"I did." When they'd returned from dinner at Jonathan's, Mr. Blackwell had gushed over what a "fine young man" he was, adding, "I couldn't have asked for a more intelligent and trustworthy man to take my son's place." Margie had stifled a gasp at that. "Have you thought about going over your father's head?" she asked.

"Many times. But when I let that scenario play out, it always ends the same way, with me being disowned, kicked out, tuition money cut off. I'll risk all that if we can't discover anything in the next week. In the meantime, we have to try."

"Then..." Margie took a steadying breath. "Then I have an idea." She repeated the slow inhale and exhale. "I'll host a Christmas party at home next weekend and invite Jonathan and Laverne to Dennison. While they're gone, you search his apartment."

Margie's boldness was rewarded by Andrea's stunned expression. As the color drained from her face, she shook her head. "How would I get in? It's a second-floor apartment. I can't just—"

Andrea's jaw appeared to unhinge when Margie held out her hand. With a single key, marked "213," resting on her palm.

CHAPTER FOURTEEN

"A re you sure you want to do this?" Janet, wearing a red T-shirt with white lettering that said, "LET IT SNOW...SOMEWHERE ELSE," punched a mound of dough.

Debbie tied the strings on a snowman-print apron. "It'll only be for a few days, and I'm pretty sure the elders didn't think of me only because I have guest rooms."

Janet looked up at her, fist still sunk in soft sweet roll dough. "You're right. I was wanting to protect you, but you could be a huge help. I take back my caution. This is a good thing."

"Thank you. Just pray we get along. It's hard for some people to accept help."

"Most people," Janet corrected. "We like to be givers. In control. I'm praying already."

Debbie picked up a stack of baskets filled with butter and jelly packets and headed for the door between the kitchen and the café then turned around. "Has Ian said anything more about Ashling?"

"Just that they're hopeful. The swelling in her brain seems to be going down. They're going to keep her in the induced coma for several more days at least. She has a few cracked ribs and a knee injury, but those aren't serious."

"I haven't heard anyone else talking about what we saw on the security camera feed. I hope that stays quiet. At least until she can give an explanation."

Janet nodded. "You said it looked like they were laughing. To me, that means it had to have been just a prank."

"I sure hope so. It's still a theft though."

"And she's eighteen. If it goes to court, she'll be tried as an adult."

That fact had already occurred to Debbie. Her heart hurt for Colleen. And Ashling. "It's so out of character for her. She's always so sweet and helpful and…" She could almost feel the glow of a light bulb in the back of her brain. "What if she had no idea it wasn't authorized? What if someone hired her to help move it? It's what she does, right?"

Janet pulled her fist out of the stainless-steel bowl. "It is. So maybe we've been on the right track all along, trying to figure out who would have a motive to steal it or remove it for some reason."

"Motive but not opportunity."

"Huh?"

"Think about it. If the Good Shepherd residents and their cohorts wanted to steal the bench, they couldn't possibly do it themselves. They'd have to hire someone younger. Much younger."

"Ah. True." Janet dumped the dough onto the table. "Everyone knows about Eileen's involvement with the depot. And Harry's. If one of them called Ashling and asked her to pick it up and deliver it somewhere, she probably wouldn't think to question them."

"Exactly." But something nagged in Debbie's brain, dimming the light bulb. "Ian said Ashling's truck was totaled. But she wasn't driving her truck in the video. She wasn't driving at all. Her truck is bigger and newer. If she was hired to do a job, wouldn't she have used her own truck and not a smaller, ancient one driven by someone else?"

"Maybe she was hired to help the person they hired."

Debbie sighed. "Or maybe she didn't want to be recognized. Her truck is bright red and has her business name on the doors."

Janet echoed her sigh. "Let's not go there. Let's assume she's innocent and keep looking for people with motives."

"If our conversations with Harry and Eileen and Madeline are any indication of what we're going to hear from the alleged Bench Bandits, I'm not too hopeful. Harry is angry about the bench going missing. Madeline says she doesn't know anything, and whatever Eileen and Ray are hiding fits in a drawer."

Other than the sneak peek before he skedaddled out of Eileen's room, Debbie hadn't seen Ray, the man she'd bought her house from, for a while.

Back in the spring, she'd had many occasions to visit him, taking things she'd found in the attic or asking questions about the old house's finicky furnace and the unique wiring configuration in the basement. Ray, a World War II veteran, seemed to enjoy the visits. "When I find out what time my Louisiana guests are arriving, I'll see if I can squeeze in a visit. That'll give me another reason to talk to anyone else who might be hanging out at Good Shepherd."

Janet floured her rolling pin and began rolling out the dough with rhythmic movements. "You know a lot of the staff, right?"

Debbie gave a slow nod. "Most of them. Why?"

"They hear things. Maybe one of them has been eavesdropping on their meetings."

"Good thinking. And if I can't find anyone who already knows something, maybe we can enlist someone to start being a little extra attentive to our Greatest Generation citizens."

"In other words, clue them in on our little espionage mission."

"Precisely."

Pastor Nick called as Debbie was walking home from work. "Sorry to get back to you so late," he apologized. "I just found out that your guests, Rachel Broussard and her daughter, Susannah, will be arriving about five o'clock. If that's too short of notice, we'd be happy to invite them to dinner and—"

"That will be perfect. Dinner is cooking as we speak, and their rooms are ready. If you and Brenda would like to join us, that would be wonderful."

"Thank you. I don't even have to ask Bren. She's anxious to meet them. What can we bring?"

"Just yourselves."

"Well, then I think I can say with confidence that we will be bringing something for their dinner tomorrow night. There was a pork roast in our slow cooker when I went home for lunch today."

"I'm sure they would appreciate that, especially when I tell them what an amazing cook Brenda is."

They said goodbye, and Debbie picked up her pace. When she got home, she sprinted up the stairs and changed into jeans and a sweater. A blast of cold air hit her as she opened the door to the attic. Did she need even more insulation than she'd had put in?

November's heating bill hadn't been too bad. What would the next three months look like?

Two cardboard boxes she'd set aside for Ray sat at the top of the stairs—all things that had been here when she moved in, and all Christmas-related. Would they bring a smile to Ray's face, or make him sad? One box contained a large Advent calendar that appeared to be made from felted wool. Across the top, appliquéd pieces of fabric and sewed-on sequins and seed pearls created a folk-art manger scene. Below that were twenty-five numbered felt pockets. Though the once-white pieces were now slightly yellowed, it was in good condition. A thin dowel rod for hanging was in the box. After finding it, she'd gone to the dollar store and bought a couple bags of candy and several trinkets, in hopes a small surprise each day would help brighten the season.

The other box contained Christmas cards, still in their envelopes. She'd peeked inside a couple but hadn't read any of them. The postmarks were from all over the country, starting in 1945. The latest she'd found was sent in 1966. She guessed many were from men Ray had served with in Europe.

As she carried the boxes down the steps, she prayed they would bring joy. It was Ray who had brought the word *bittersweet* into her almost daily vocabulary. Not for the first time, she wondered who it was that first coined the word that encompassed so much of the last twenty years for her. Maybe it was time to focus more on the sweet part. And maybe bringing a bit of sweetness to Ray Zink was the next step toward that goal.

On the way to Good Shepherd, she thought about who on the staff she should "clue in," and how she should word it.

Ray was playing the piano in the dayroom when she walked in. Eileen and Madeline were both part of his audience of eight residents and a couple of staff members. Ray nodded and smiled at her but didn't stop playing. The Christmas carols had everyone chiming in. He finished "Have Yourself a Merry Little Christmas," and then, without a pause, launched into "Here We Come a-Caroling."

Debbie recognized Lorena Williams, her first-grade teacher, in the group. She knew from her father's reports that Lorena's dementia had advanced to the point where she didn't remember her own children and mostly sat with her hands folded and a faraway expression on her face. Yet here she was, smiling and singing "Love and joy come to you and to you glad Christmas too…" Debbie knew science had explanations for this music-memory phenomenon, but she also knew God was the creator of everything science set out to discover. Was Ray aware of the little miracle his music was producing?

After setting the boxes on an empty chair, Debbie walked over to the three women wearing lanyards. She greeted them all then stood next to the one she knew by name. She'd gone to school with Sonya, who was now an RN and recently returned to work after her youngest graduated high school. Sonya smiled. "He's amazing, isn't he?"

"Sure is." In more ways than she could put into words. After Reed died, Ray had written her a letter. She'd received several from veterans, some she'd never met. Though she knew him only as an acquaintance of her grandfather at the time, his letter was one she'd kept. It was still in the white box, and she reread it every year. Heartfelt and written from a soul that had known deep loss, it spoke to her pain and yet offered hope. Though he'd shared a few of his stories from the war with her, she knew there was likely much he had never shared with anyone.

"He could so easily have become bitter and let the music stop," Sonya said.

But he chose the sweet over the bitter. "Yes." Debbie turned to stare at Sonya. Was she, also, speaking from a place of pain? Was Sonya the one she should take into her confidence about her suspicions? She was about to ask if they could move to a quieter place to chat when Ray stopped playing. His fans clapped, and he bowed then looked at Debbie. "Are those for me?" he mouthed.

She nodded then told Sonya she'd like to talk to her after she was done visiting with Ray. She picked up the boxes and walked over to the piano. Ray lifted his hands. "Let a he-man carry those for you." He grinned at his own humor and set the boxes on his lap.

"Want me to drive?" Debbie asked.

"Sure. Since I'm doing all the heavy lifting, I'll give in. In my heyday, it was only the wild girls who could drive, you know."

Stepping behind him, she took hold of the padded handles on his wheelchair. "That's me. I'm a wild one."

He laughed as he tapped the boxes. "What did you find now?"

"A few more Christmas things. Even if you don't have room for them, I thought you might like to see them. Actually, I have a selfish reason for bringing them." She told him about gathering Christmas stories. "I was hoping maybe looking at old Christmas cards would spark some memories."

"Memories are all I've got these days, kiddo. And there's not much I enjoy more than sharing them."

She turned into his room and angled his chair so he could face her, almost knee-to-knee when she sat in his wingback guest chair, and also have a view of the sunset. She took the box with the wall hanging and opened it for him.

He reached out with knobby, blotched hands. Hands that had fought in combat but could coax joy from piano keys. He stroked the fabric. "My mother made this back during the Great Depression. We didn't have money for fabric and such, so she cut up an old red jacket. She'd wrap up little pieces of fudge or raisins, sometimes a small toy or a penny. It seemed to make the wait for Christmas a little easier."

He lifted it. "It's heavy." Suddenly, a smile broke across his face, and Debbie caught a glimpse of childlike delight. He tapped on the pocket marked 7 then opened the flap and pulled out a wrapped square of milk chocolate. His eyes glistened, and for a moment she thought he might break down, but instead, he placed his hand on hers. "Thank you."

He unwrapped the chocolate, put it in his mouth, and nodded with contentment. After a moment, he pointed to a spot on the wall next to the foot of his bed. "I'll ask someone to hang it right there." Then he tapped the shoebox on his lap. "Christmas cards?"

"Yes. I save some of mine too, and I like to look back at them. I didn't know if that would be fun for you or…" She left the sentence hanging.

"Or painful?"

"Yes."

"Most things in life have a bit of both, don't they? Let's go through these and hunt for the fun." With hands that trembled slightly, he pulled out three envelopes. "My glasses are over there."

He pointed to his bedside table. "But maybe you'd like to read them to me." He winked at her.

"I'd love to." She took the envelopes. "Which one should I open first? These are all from 1946." She took a moment to let that sink in. She held little pieces of history in her hands. "There's one from the Schmidts in Austin, Texas, one from Jack Southern in Portland, and one from the Blackwells in Ravenna."

Ravenna. Where had she just heard the name?

"That one. Margie always writes such newsy Christmas letters."

Margie. Her pulse ramped up a notch. "How do you know them?"

"We grew up together. Margie McGarry and her brother, Dutch, lived two houses down from me, and Jesse Blackwell and his sister Andrea were just a block away. As kids, we were thick as thieves, as they say. I was the one who told Jesse, way back in sixth grade, that he was going to marry Margie. Turns out I was right."

CHAPTER FIFTEEN

*J*esse and Dutch enlisted on the same day in 1942. I was wishing I could go with them, but I had to wait until June of '43, my eighteenth birthday. As you know, that turned out in my favor." He gave a wistful smile, and his comment about everything in life having a bit of joy and pain replayed in her mind. A few months ago, she'd learned all about his one true love, a woman he'd only spent a few months with before he enlisted but never forgot. Though he'd had years of heartache, wondering why Eleanor O'Reilly hadn't waited for him, he'd declared he'd do it all over again even if he knew the outcome ahead of time.

"Jesse and Margie were just good friends at the time, but they wrote back and forth. It was my opinion that they'd been in love with each other for years but didn't know it until they finally put it into words in those letters." Ray ran his fingertips across the tops of the envelopes in the box. "The power of the written word, you know. Anyway, as God's timing would have it, we all got leave in December of '43. Jesse proposed with that old bench, Margie said yes, and we all stood up at their wedding." His expression sobered. "And then we went back."

Men. Why did they always leave out the romantic details? "Harry said the bench came on the train."

"Yep. Dutch and I had already been home for a few days, and we were hiding out behind the depot. You shoulda seen Margie's face when that bench got unloaded. And then Jesse hopped off the train, and she just kinda collapsed like a melting snowman. It was a sight to behold."

"But then he had to go back? Where was he stationed?"

"In France at the time. They had a week together. Lots of couples had quick weddings like that. Some didn't know each other as well as Jesse and Margie did. Some had only a few hours for a honeymoon, and that was all they ever got." Ray closed his eyes for a moment then opened them and gazed at her. "I don't have to tell you about that kind of heartbreak, do I?"

Debbie swallowed hard. "No." She needed to get back to Jesse and Margie's story before she got too emotional. "I've heard some things about Margie. People think she was involved in some kind of spying."

A small smile deepened the creases on Ray's face. "Yes, she was. But I can't give you any details. Not because I'm withholding, but because I don't know. She was given a commendation from the US Army, but I never heard the details."

"Did you ever ask?" She knew the question was a bit too blatant, but she wasn't sure how to phrase it differently.

"Sure did. I asked Margie and Jesse. And Andrea, Jesse's sister. She was involved in it somehow. I gather it was something big." His smile widened. "You know, it's been a couple decades since I bugged them about it. Maybe they're free to talk now."

"So they're both still…"

"Yep. Jesse had a stroke a few months back, so he's not mobile anymore. I try to talk to him every couple of weeks. He tires easily, but he can still carry on a conversation. Margie's still got all her wits about her." He patted the arm of his chair. "Like me, she's got wheels now. I used to get up to see them on a regular basis, but now that this is the only vehicle I'm allowed to operate, it's been a while. They've got great-grandkids living here in town, but it's been some years since they were able to come down for a visit. They used to come in December and have their picture taken on the bench. Kinda hoping they don't hear about the bench going missing."

"I'd love to meet them. Do you think they'd be open to telling me their story? The romance part, I mean."

Ray took a moment to answer. "I think they might. Margie's hearing's not the greatest. If you could meet with her in person, she'd love that."

"They're still living in Ravenna?"

"Yep. In a place like this. They have adjoining rooms. Margie spends most of her day by Jesse's side." His eyes clouded for a moment, and then he pointed to a small brown notebook sitting on his desk. "Get Margie's number out of that." He lifted one finger of the hand resting on the box of letters. "Last I knew, they still had all the letters they'd written to each other during the war. Those letters would make a great book."

"I bet they would." But would Margie be willing to share them with a stranger?

Ray stifled a yawn, and Debbie apologized for leading him on a rabbit trail instead of reading the cards she held in her hand.

He shook his head. "This was fun. It's about time for my second nap, but I got more stories for you whenever you come back."

She took the box and set it on his bedside table. "I'll make a point of doing that soon." She patted his shoulder then found Margie's name in the address book and took a picture of it. "I'll see you in a day or two."

In the parking lot, she called Paulette and asked if she'd be willing to work the next day as well as Saturday. Ravenna was a bit out of the way, but she could stop there on her way to Cleveland. It wouldn't help her find the bench, but hopefully she'd end up with a story…the origin story of the Dennison depot bench.

On her way out, she found Sonya. How was she going to word this? With a deep breath, she said in a conspiratorial whisper, "I think some of the older residents are planning some kind of a Christmas surprise. I'm not exactly sure what, but if you hear anything, would you let me know? I'd like to help if I can. Anonymously."

Sonya nodded. "They have been rather secretive about something lately." She glanced over at Eileen, dozing in a wingback chair with a book on her lap. "I'll keep you posted."

The house smelled of sage and onion when Debbie walked in the door. She hoped it would be welcoming to her guests. Using two forks, she eased the cooked chicken onto a platter to let it cool. Then she measured out flour, salt, and baking powder and cut in a stick of butter until the small white lumps were uniform in size. She formed the dough into a ball, rolled it out, and used a biscuit cutter she'd inherited from her grandmother to cut circles from the three-quarter-inch-high dough.

When the biscuits were almost done, she started on dessert. She'd taken a bag of sliced apples out of the freezer before work, and they'd thawed just enough in the fridge, with a few ice crystals keeping them firm. She dumped them in a square pan, poured a half cup of sugar over them then mixed softened butter, brown sugar, cinnamon, and rolled oats, sprinkled the mixture on the apples, and slid it into the preheated oven.

As she worked, she thought about her booklet idea. What would she call it? *Christmas in Dennison* seemed the most logical, though it wasn't all that catchy. Maybe something better would come to her while she conducted interviews. She planned to keep it simple. A small booklet, one she could copy and assemble herself.

Her timer went off for the apple crisp, and her phone rang at the same moment. Janet. Debbie said hi while pulling the bubbling pan of apples with crunchy topping from the oven.

"I have some maybe good news. Tiffany just called. She's been talking to Colleen a couple times a day. They're going to try bringing Ashling out of her coma tomorrow. The doctors are hopeful the swelling will stay down. We need to be praying."

"Definitely. This has to be so hard for Tiff."

"She's a mess. Which brings me to a favor."

"Anything."

"I know you'll have Betsy with you, but is there any chance you'd have room to bring Tiff home with you on Sunday? Tomorrow's her last day of classes. We'll have to get her back for finals on Wednesday, but I think she just needs to be here."

"Absolutely. I'll text her, and we'll arrange it. Selfishly, that's a bit of a blessing. By Sunday I'll be more than ready for a new topic of conversation. I hope it doesn't sound crass, but I think it might be good for Betsy to focus on someone else's needs."

"I hope it works out that way. For good, I mean. Are you ready for company?"

Debbie gave a slightly shaky sigh. "I think so. At least the house and dinner are ready. I'm a little nervous."

"That's understandable. Just try to have fun."

"I will." After hanging up, she walked into the living room and turned on the porch and yard lights then stood in the room lit only by a fire in the fireplace, the tiny white lights on her tree, and the candles lining the fireplace mantel. Through the archway to her right, the table was set with white stoneware plates and red cloth napkins that coordinated with the pine ring accented with shiny red apples surrounding a pillar candle. She hoped it wasn't over the top. Her goal was casual with a touch of elegance—something to make Rachel and Susannah feel special, yet at home.

At ten to five, she heard a car drive up. Her stomach tightened until she recognized the car. Pastor Nick and Brenda. Most of the tension that had built in the last hour whooshed out on a heavy sigh. She opened the door, took two stacked containers from Brenda, and then gave her a one-armed hug. "I'm so glad you got here first. I'll put these in the kitchen and then take your coats."

Pastor Nick said from behind Brenda, "I'll keep mine so I can help carry bags."

Debbie smiled at him. She wished she had a bit more of his servant heart.

A few minutes later they settled on the leather furniture, and Debbie asked if they'd heard the latest news about Ashling. Pastor Nick nodded. "Colleen called just as we left the house. I hope they can wake her safely. This has been a hard week."

"Do you think Colleen will be able to care for her after she gets home? Ian said she has cracked ribs and a knee injury." What she really wondered, but couldn't ask, was whether or not Ashling would even be released into the care of her grandmother. Would she be arrested for her part in stealing the bench?

Brenda shook her head. "We went to see her yesterday to assess the situation, thinking maybe we could hire a live-in caregiver."

Debbie felt a sense of relief that they didn't seem to have any doubts about her coming home when she was able to. Surely, if Colleen had heard about Ashling's involvement, she would have shared that with her pastor. "If home care doesn't work out, Good Shepherd's rehab wing is excellent. I know I'm biased, but I've heard other people say the same."

"I would agree. I got great care there a few years ago."

"That's right. I forgot about your surgery."

He put his hand on his lower back. "Old war injury, you know." He grinned.

Brenda laughed. "The only war this man fought in was in the church nursery. He was picking up a toddler, and he felt something pop."

"I remember that now. Mom told me about the razzing you took."

"We all have our crosses to bear. Mine is humiliation."

The sound of a car door interrupted their laughter. All three rose to their feet and walked to the front door. Pastor Nick went out and greeted the two women then helped them carry in their bags. Four bags. It hit Debbie with sudden force that those two bags each might contain everything they owned. She stepped out of the entryway and waited on the porch. Pastor Nick made introductions and then Rachel and Susannah came into the house. Before they even walked through the glass doors leading to the living room, Rachel gasped and began to cry.

Without thinking twice, Debbie wrapped her arms around her. Over Rachel's shaking shoulder, she saw Brenda put an arm around Susannah, whose eyes were brimming with tears.

Rachel didn't pull away. Debbie prayed quietly, asking God to bring her comfort. What was she thinking? That they didn't belong here? That they should have found a place closer to home? Was it that they missed everything they'd left behind? Or maybe they were simply physically and emotionally exhausted.

Pastor Nick found the tissues she kept on an end table and held them out. Rachel's sobs quieted, and she pulled away and took several from the box. She wiped her face and blew her nose. "Th-this is just…beyond anything we could have hoped for. This last month has been so, so hard. But this feels…like coming home."

December 13, 1942

Margie stood in the front hallway, staring down at the black telephone receiver in her hand, a hand that trembled. She'd had the bus ride home from Ravenna to think about her plans to host a party and invite Jonathan and Laverne to Dennison. But it wasn't going to work. She went back over the conversation.

Laverne had said, "Oh, I wish we could, but we're heading out of town for the weekend. I need to do some Christmas shopping, and Jonathan loves to draw. Did I tell you that already? Especially buildings and bridges. It's supposed to snow this weekend, so he wants to take some pictures of bridges that he can work on drawing over the winter. Where did you say you live?" When Margie told her again, Laverne had answered with, "That sounds familiar. Let me go talk to him." Margie waited, staring down at the overnight bag at her feet, wondering when she'd pack it again. And then Laverne came back to the phone. "Yeah, sorry, we won't be able to make it, but thanks for the invite. Toodles." And she'd hung up.

Setting the receiver in its cradle, Margie drew in a long, slow breath to steady her nerves. She needed to call Andrea, but first she needed to think. Her parents were starting to ask questions. Why the need for all the long-distance calls when she and Andrea had been content to write letters since Andrea had moved? Did she have a love interest in Ravenna? Was Andrea doing something illegal by letting her use a government-issued bus pass?

The house would be quiet for another hour. Her parents were at the Sunday night service at church. She needed that hour to pray. She picked up her bag and headed for the stairs, strategizing as she went. Andrea had the key to Jonathan and Laverne's apartment. They would be gone for the weekend, which meant Andrea could still follow through. But could she, in good conscience, let Andrea take that risk alone? "Lord, I need wisdom."

CHAPTER SIXTEEN

It felt strange to not be in a hurry on a Friday morning. Debbie awakened before the time her alarm would normally buzz and took things slow, enjoying a cup of coffee in front of the lit Christmas tree. By six she had two pans of seven-layer bars in the oven, enough for the cookie exchange at Stephanie's with some to leave at home for her guests.

She was in the kitchen cutting up strawberries when her phone rang. Janet. She glanced at the clock. Six thirty. The café would open in thirty minutes. Why was Janet calling? "Miss me already?"

"I know you're leaving soon and you've got company, but is there any chance you can stop by the café for a few minutes on your way out of town? I was sure I'd ordered more sheet pans than what we've been using, so I went hunting in the storeroom, and I found something."

"Something? Are you going to give me a clue?"

"No. I don't even know for sure what's on it, and I won't lis… check it out until you get here."

"That's just plain mean. Of course I'm coming in now. I'll be there in about an hour."

"Good. See you then." Janet gave a spooky laugh that could have come from an old monster movie.

Debbie had topped the berries, in individual fluted glasses, with whipped cream when Rachel came up the basement stairs in a robe and slippers. "Good morning." Debbie pointed to the coffeepot, and her guest gave a grateful nod. "How did you sleep?"

"Better than I have in over a month. Thank you." Her tone of voice clearly encompassed far more than just a comfortable bed.

Debbie handed her a cup of coffee then checked the sausage, egg, and cheese bake in the oven. "This needs a few more minutes." She gestured toward the table, and they sat kitty-corner from each other. "I hope Susannah can sleep late. Is she still in high school?"

"No. She graduated last year. She'd had a month at cosmetology school when our world turned upside down."

"I can't imagine…"

Rachel picked up her coffee mug and held it in both hands. "I think maybe you can. Some of it anyway. Aunt Sara told me you lost your fiancé."

Debbie's initial reaction was to downplay her grief, to say something about it not comparing to the pain of losing a husband of maybe twenty years or more, but something stopped her, and she simply nodded. "The best advice I got was from a World War II veteran who lost a lot of friends in battle. Shortly after my fiancé's funeral, I got a letter from him that said, 'Let Jesus and His people carry you until you feel ready to stand on your own.' And they did."

Rachel blinked back tears. "That's beautiful. And now you're doing that for us." She pressed a napkin to her eyes. "I would have had an amazing support system, but none of us were in a position to hold each other up."

"I hope you'll find that here."

"The kinship of God's people is incredible. My father was in the navy, and we moved a lot. I remember my mother telling me that if you know the Lord, you can find sisters on any continent."

"Makes you wonder how people cope without those connections."

Rachel nodded. "My husband and I had only been married a little over a year when Katrina hit. We lived in a two-bedroom apartment, but we took in a couple with a baby who'd lost their home. I never thought we'd ever be the ones…"

Debbie slid her hand over Rachel's just as the oven timer beeped. She squeezed the thin hand and rose. "I feel kind of bad about leaving right after you got here, but maybe that's exactly what you both need. You'll have the weekend to settle in and rest up. I'll give you my number, and I'll be a phone call away if you need anything. I'll also leave my friend Janet's number. She helped me unpack when I moved in, so she knows where everything is, and she can be here in a minute if need be. And even if you don't need anything, she'll probably stop by this afternoon with a box of doughnuts and cinnamon rolls." She smiled as Rachel's eyes lit. "Speaking of food, there are leftovers from last night and the pork roast Brenda brought in the fridge. Knowing her, she'll be checking on you every day to see if you need anything."

"I gathered that. She and Pastor Nick have already done so much. They're going to pick us up for church on Sunday. Are there any girls around Susannah's age? She was so involved in the young adult ministry back home, and she was on the prayer team and taking training for a suicide prevention hotline." Rachel didn't need to explain more. The worry on her face spoke volumes.

Debbie lifted the pan out of the oven and set it on a wood trivet on the table. "I know of a couple of kids. I can ask Brenda to introduce her, but the very best person for that job is my friend Janet's daughter. I'm bringing her back from college on Sunday for a couple of days before finals, and she could use a friend right now." She told Rachel about Ashling, leaving out the part she couldn't tell.

"How sad. Her family must be distraught."

"Her mother and father aren't in the picture, at least right now. She was raised by her grandmother, and I'm sure the stress is getting to her though she's blessed with the kind of support we were just talking about." As Debbie picked up a knife to cut into the casserole, she marveled at God's timing. "Some people would call it coincidence, but look at God's hand in this. Tiffany wasn't planning on coming home until after finals. She's only coming home because of Ashling's accident. And then God brings you and Susannah here. Two girls who each need a friend, and maybe He'll use both of them to be part of the support Ashling's going to need."

Rachel closed her eyes, and a tear slid down her cheek. "His mysterious, beautiful ways."

Debbie was pulling out of her driveway when her phone rang. She answered with a smile. "Morning, Greg."

"Good morning. What time are you leaving?"

"I'm actually on my way now, but I have to stop at the café first. Janet found something in the storeroom she can't wait to show me, but she won't give me any hints."

"That's just cruel. Something about the bench?"

"I'm assuming so. Or about the first couple to have their initials carved on it. Did I tell you we found out their names?"

"I heard you or Janet mention Margie McGarry."

"Her fiancé, and eventually husband, is Jesse Blackwell. I'm leaving early to meet them. Jesse proposed by gifting Margie the bench, and then they got married at Christmas here in Dennison, so I want to add their story to my booklet."

"Booklet?"

It had only been three days since she'd talked to him. Thinking of all that had happened since then made her head spin. "I guess we have some catching up to do."

"That's kind of why I called. I didn't know you were leaving early. I was going to ask if you had time to go out for coffee before you head to Cleveland."

"Oh." Coffee. Was *that* a date? "I would have loved to if this opportunity to talk to Margie hadn't come up. Rain check?"

"Of course."

She told him about her idea to compile the memories of Christmas in Dennison. "And I guess I didn't get a chance to tell you I have people living at my house."

By the time she finished telling him about Rachel and Susannah, she was parking in front of the depot.

He started to say goodbye then said, "Oh! I almost forgot the other reason I called. I talked to the president of the furniture company. He said Michael Morgan has been on vacation in Aruba for the past two weeks."

"So if he was involved, it was indirectly."

"Looks that way. At least we can be sure it wasn't him in the video. I imagine the police already figured that out, but I haven't heard anything."

She thanked him for the information, and he ended the call by saying he'd be praying for her trip. "Thank you. That means a lot." *Much more than you could ever imagine.*

Inside the café door, Debbie took a moment to survey the scene as if she were a first-time customer. All but one table was full. The hum of conversations dispersed by laughter was a sound that felt, in Rachel's words, like coming home. Paulette sashayed around the end of the counter with three giant plated muffins. She greeted Debbie with a smile. The kitchen door opened, and Janet came out with a tray in each hand. Carrot cake muffins were on the board as today's special. A combo of carrots, raisins, pineapple, coconut, and walnuts with a surprise filling of sweetened cream cheese. Debbie stepped behind the counter. "I'll take three to go."

Janet, eyes on the tray in her left hand, startled. Debbie reached out and steadied both trays. "What's got you so jumpy?"

"Waiting for you." Grinning, Janet set the trays on the counter then called to Paulette. "I'll be back in a few minutes." Untying her apron as she walked, she motioned for Debbie to come.

Debbie followed her to the museum side. "This must be good."

"I hope it is. It will definitely be interesting." Janet stopped at an old portable phonograph on display and picked up a square brown envelope.

Even before reading the words across the bottom, Debbie knew exactly what she was looking at. It wasn't the first time they'd found

Voice-O-Graph records. Some here in the depot, and one, the one that had touched her heart the most, up in her attic. A record made for Ray from Eleanor, his long-lost love. She zeroed in on the return address, and her pulse jumped the way Janet had when she'd startled her. *Pvt. J. W. Blackwell.*

Jesse.

The envelope was dated December 6, 1942, and was addressed to the depot but in care of Miss Margie McGarry.

"This could be a love letter," she said.

Janet nodded then slowly pulled the laminated cardboard record out of its sleeve. Carefully, she lifted the needle on the phonograph and slid the disk onto the turntable.

This wouldn't be a long message. Debbie thought back to her few and far between video calls with Reed. They'd had at least ten minutes each time to catch up. Jesse Blackwell, on the other hand, would have been sitting alone in a booth at an arcade or some tourist attraction, maybe even at the top of the Empire State Building before shipping out, and he would have had only sixty-five seconds to say what he wanted to say. She held her breath as the needle began to pick up a staticky sound…a sound recorded decades ago.

> "Hi Margie,
>
> "I'm so sorry about the way we met on Friday. If you followed through, and I have every confidence that you did, someone has probably gotten in touch with you, and you know why I was so upset. Knowing you, you're going to want to get involved. I desperately want to say please don't, because this is just so complicated, but we need someone from the

outside that we can trust. This may be your chance to follow in the steps of the heroines in those books you always read, or like your Marie Walcamp in all of her adventures. Please, be careful. Speaking of books, I happen to know that David King's friend's favorite story is the Trojan Horse. You might keep that in mind as you are preparing for Christmas. I will write more. Please share my letters with the one who knows the way we did things as kids. I don't dare communicate directly. Well, I only have twelve seconds now to say thank you and I'm sorry to involve you. Merry Christmas. I meant it when I said I would make it up to you. Planning the ways will keep me going.

"Love, Jesse."

CHAPTER SEVENTEEN

*A*s she drove north out of Dennison, Debbie tried to remember phrases from the Voice-O-Graph recording. Janet had played it a second time, and they had recorded it on their phones so they could analyze it together later. 1942. According to Harry and Ray, that was a year before the bench was delivered. The envelope was dated December 6, and Jesse and Margie had met on the Friday before. She wished she'd taken the time to look on her phone for a December 1942 calendar.

What was Jesse asking Margie to do, or hoping she would do, even though it was "complicated"? He'd mentioned heroines like Marie Walcamp. Debbie and Janet had met each other's eyes at that moment. Could there be a clue in one of Marie's movies? And what had he meant by sharing his letters with "the one who knows the way we did things as kids"?

She'd hoped Margie would show her some of Jesse's letters. She wanted to know about their love story. Now, she had a much more important reason to ask to see them. If Margie, born and raised in Dennison, had been a true war hero, her story needed to be recorded before she was gone. In just a few years there would be no one left to tell the firsthand stories of the Greatest Generation. That knowledge gave Debbie the feeling of trying to hold a handful of sand, unable to keep the grains from sifting through her fingers.

The hour-and-fifteen-minute drive gave her time to put her thoughts in order. She pictured all the information she'd gathered in the past week like the papers that once cluttered her desk. She needed to sort them into nice, neat, manageable piles. One would be labeled "Café," and include the plans for the Grinch party. Another would be labeled "Bench," and a third came under the category "Personal." That one held her time with Betsy, the party at Steph's, ways she could help Rachel and Susannah, and…Greg. Maybe he needed his own separate pile.

She started with the café. Though it would have been much easier to hire a caterer for the party, they'd decided to do the cooking themselves. Janet had found tons of ideas online, and they'd come up with their menu. Yesterday, Debbie had printed it out and posted it at the café.

Grinch Kabobs
Roast Beast
Who Hash
Mount Crumpit Noodles
Grinch Greens
Cindy Lu Salad
Whobillation Cake
Max Trax Ice Cream

Their dishes had created quite a stir and a lot of questions. Exactly what they'd hoped for. She'd had to reassure several customers that it was all, indeed, edible. Though they'd wanted to keep the actual menu a secret, she'd given in and explained to a few that

Ian would be smoking brisket for their "roast beast" and that Grinch Kabobs were made from fruit. She and Janet had loved the picture of the adorable little appetizers assembled on toothpicks with a green grape for the head topped by Santa hats made from a slice of banana, half a strawberry, and a mini marshmallow. Who Hash was a medley of root vegetables, Mount Crumpit Noodles would be wide egg noodles with a garlic butter sauce, and the cake and ice cream recipes were yet to be decided but would be delicious.

Were they starting a lasting tradition? Maybe next year they'd host the same party but without the drama of a missing bench. That thought led her to Ashling, and she took a moment to pray for her complete healing…and forgiveness and grace if needed. "Lord, if she did this intentionally, I pray people will be kind. She's so young."

As I-77 took her past Bolivar, she switched to the "Bench" pile. It felt like they were in a holding pattern, waiting for Ashling to wake up. She hated to think that the girl might be spending her recovery time with a sentence hanging over her head. Would Ian give her a few days after she regained consciousness before starting to question her? She wished they could just forget everything that had happened. The bench was only a thing. In the big picture, it really wasn't all that important. But any way she looked at it, everything still came down to one fact. It was a theft. Ashling had been involved in stealing property that belonged to the Village of Dennison.

They needed to find answers before the news about Ashling's involvement became public. There was one strategy they hadn't yet tried. The straightforward approach. What if she were to just come right out and ask Eileen or Ray if they knew anything about Ashling helping someone take the bench? Whether they had a part in it or not, she knew they could be trusted not to spread the news. Maybe all it would take was a phone call and she'd know the truth in moments. She pulled off at the next exit, parked at a gas station, and tapped on the number for Good Shepherd. "Hi, this is Debbie Albright. Could you connect me to Eileen Palmer's room, please?" She waited through several rings and then heard a voice she wasn't expecting.

Kim. What was Kim doing there in the middle of the morning? Come to think of it, she hadn't seen her when she stopped at the café. "Hi, Kim, I have a question for your mom. Is everything all right?"

"Everything's fine. I'm taking her to an eye doctor appointment this morning. Helping her get her coat on now. Anything I can relay to her?"

"Nothing urgent." Though it did feel like it was, she wasn't going to tell Kim to flat out ask her mother if she had a hand in Ashling taking the bench without authorization. "I'll talk to her when I get back."

Beyond the question of Ashling's motivation, she did have other questions that were beginning to feel urgent. The stories she'd heard in the past few days had whetted her appetite for more.

Margie McGarry was the same age as Eileen. Knowing people who had lived through a century of change was such a gift, and she was privileged to know several of them. The wealth of knowledge and experience and...she kept going back to the word...*wisdom* was staggering. She thought of the boys who'd eagerly listened to Harry's stories, and then her mind went to Julian. He'd been enthralled by the pictures of Marie Walcamp.

Heroes. Kids today still needed to hear about heroes. Real, true heroes. Flawed people who stepped up and did the right thing at the right time in spite of obstacles. When she finished her Christmas memories booklet, maybe someday she'd think about putting together another one with the collective wisdom of her senior friends.

When she reached the assisted living home where Margie lived, she turned off the car and sat in silence for several minutes. Vista Veranda was a welcoming place, with white pillars supporting the overhang near the entrance, wreaths on the front doors, and cut-out snowflakes on many of the windows.

She hadn't called ahead for fear that she might be turned away. Though she and Margie likely had many friends in common, they were strangers. When she finally felt calm enough, she picked up her purse, the box containing three carrot cake muffins, and the Voice-O-Graph, and walked in.

Like Good Shepherd, the atmosphere was homey. Brick fireplace, gleaming oak floors, two-tone tan walls with white trim, comfortable furniture, and a tall tree covered in white lights, silver and blue ribbons, and satin balls. But, unlike the place where Eileen and Ray lived, there was no mistaking that this was the next step, the place that filled the gap between retirement home and nursing home. Here, she had to sign in just inside the door. While the staff at Good Shepherd were recognized by the lanyards they wore around their necks or clipped to belts, here the staff wore scrubs.

"Good morning!" A bright voice greeted her from a corner desk.

"Hi. I'm wondering if Margie Blackwell is free for a short visit." Realizing she probably needed to give a bit more information, she said, "My name is Debbie Albright. I'm from her hometown. I've never met Margie, but I'm a friend of a friend, Ray Zink, and—"

The round-faced woman with glasses on a gold chain stood. "Any friend of Ray's is someone Margie would love to see. I'll take

WHISTLE STOP CAFÉ MYSTERIES

you to her. How is Ray? He used to come in often. Sometimes he'd play the piano for us. Such an inspiration. I would introduce him to some of our residents who couldn't seem to get past their physical limitations." She led Debbie around a corner and into a long hallway. "His joie de vivre was contagious." The woman stopped and held out her hand. "Excuse my manners. I'm Calista Owens. I've worked here since we opened. Don't tell anyone"—she used one hand to shield her mouth—"but Margie and Jesse are two of my favorites."

"From what I've heard, they've had quite a life together. Romance and intrigue, the kind of stuff movies are made of."

"Oh yes. We've heard some stories. But I think there's a whole lot they're keeping secret too."

So maybe Calista wasn't going to be the one to answer her biggest questions. "I'm collecting Christmas memories from some of our older residents in Dennison. It's sad that so much of what they've experienced gets lost. People in town say Margie and a friend of hers did something heroic around Christmastime during World War II, but I haven't been able to find any details."

"Good luck getting any details out of her. She has a framed commendation signed by President Eisenhower, but whenever we ask her about it, she just says something like, "Jesse and my friend Andrea get the credit for that. I only did what anyone would to protect my town and my country."

My town? Was that a general statement, or did she actually do something to protect Dennison?

"Let's check the dayroom first. She might be in there making Christmas cards." Calista gestured to a room with large windows that flooded the area with light even on a cloudy December day. They approached the entrance. "There she is."

The woman Calista nodded toward sat at the end of a long table taking up the middle of the room. She held up a black card with a snowman made from circles of white paper, laughed, and pointed at the snowman's head, which was tilting to one side. "I think Frosty was out too late last night."

The five women and two men sitting around the table joined in her laughter. Debbie liked her immediately. Something about the way her entire face crinkled when she laughed let Debbie know she was one of those women who hadn't become a sweet little old lady just by getting old. But there was something more than sweetness there. This woman had a bit of fire in her too.

Calista approached the group at the table, and Debbie followed. Calista put her hand on Margie's shoulder. "Margie, there's someone here who would like to meet you." Her elevated voice reminded Debbie what Ray had said about Margie's hearing.

As Margie's eyes met hers, there was a moment of question in her gaze. Wariness. And then, she flashed a smile that encompassed her entire countenance. "You must be Debbie."

Debbie stopped in her tracks. "How did you know...?"

"Ray called this morning. He wanted to warn me about you." She winked and laughed. "Let's go to my room where we can talk." She glanced up at Calista. "Would you mind being my engine, dear?"

Debbie stepped forward. "I can do that. Ray has given me driving instructions."

Margie laughed again and looked at Calista. "We need to get him up here for our wheelchair races."

Calista rolled her eyes. "If we do, you better take those upper body strengthening exercises seriously. I think he's got a bit of an edge on you."

"Well, he is just a kid."

They all laughed at that. Following Margie's directions, Debbie wheeled the chair out of the room and down the hall.

"Can I get either of you anything?" Calista asked when they walked through the door of a cozy little two-room apartment. "Coffee, tea, water?"

"I'm fine," Debbie answered.

"How about a cappuccino?" Margie suggested. "Calista makes the best."

"Well, I guess I can't refuse that. But I work at a café, and it just feels wrong to have someone waiting on me."

Margie nodded. "I happen to know you do more than work there. I keep tabs on what's happening in my old hometown." She told Calista about the café in the depot where she used to volunteer.

Debbie couldn't have asked for a better segue, but she wondered what else Margie knew. Ray had hoped she wouldn't hear about the bench, and Debbie was determined not to mention it. But if she already knew it was missing…

When Calista left, Debbie positioned Margie's chair so that it faced a plush gray love seat. The room was decorated in gray and white with accents of red in Christmas-print pillows and a small tree decorated with bright red apples. Margie nodded at a closed door. "My husband is sleeping, but he wears earplugs so my visitors can shout at me."

Once settled with a fuzzy corduroy pillow behind her, Debbie said, "Anything you'd like to know about what's going on in Dennison?"

"Yes. The first thing I need to know is what you've heard about our great-granddaughter."

"Your great-granddaughter? I'm sorry. I don't think I know her."

"Ashling Kelly? I thought for sure everyone in—"

"Ashling is your…" Debbie's brain seemed to seize, as if gears were locking. Ashling was related to Margie and Jesse?

Were the two stories she was chasing down one and the same?

December 15, 1942

Margie sat in the depot at a makeshift table made from plywood and two sawhorses. The table that was often laden with trays of sandwiches, bowls of fruit, and stacks of fresh-made doughnuts was now covered with newsprint and laden with bowls of eggs.

Eggs. Again.

She grimaced at the thought of pressing her lips to them and blowing out the raw, slippery goo. But Linda March's enthusiasm was contagious, and Margie wanted to be supportive. She'd survived the first round of egg ornaments. She would get through this one too. She did have to admit that she loved watching big, strong soldiers picking up the delicate decorations and choosing just the right one for someone they loved. When a couple of the older women had offered to pack them in boxes filled with excelsior and mail them, she knew this was going to become something monumental.

Their eggstravaganza team had doubled since the first time they'd made the ornaments, so Linda gave instructions again. As she talked, Margie picked up her needle and began to chip a tiny hole in the top of an egg and a little bit larger one in the bottom. And then came the part she dreaded. "Be careful of your ears, dears," Linda called out. Then she giggled. Margie locked eyes with Eileen Turner, one of the other volunteers, and they both grimaced. After releasing a sigh, she held the egg to her mouth and began to blow out the contents. After several seconds, her efforts were rewarded with a satisfying plop. *She set the empty shell on a tray, and one of the lucky women who had perfected chipping out a large oval hole in the side without shattering the shell picked it up and took it to the other end of the table. If Margie possessed even a tiny bit of artistic talent, she might be sitting with the painters or sculptors, but, alas, up until two weeks ago, her main contribution to the war effort was sandwich making and smiling.*

"McGarry!" Molly strode across the waiting area, her booming voice echoing off the ceiling. "Mail." She thrust a square brown envelope at her, forcing Margie to drop her needle to grab it.

"Thank—" The last word got stuck in her throat as she stared at the envelope. Along the bottom were the words, Don't Write...Record It On The Voice-O-Graph. *In the return address space in the upper left corner it said,* A voice letter from Pvt. J. W. Blackwell, *and in the faintest letters, penciled under the address, she read,* Keeping my promise.

CHAPTER EIGHTEEN

argie was Ashling's great-grandmother.

As Margie stared at her, expectantly waiting for news, Debbie forced her brain to form words. "My friend Janet…her daughter is one of Ashling's best friends. And Ashling is a frequent customer at the café." She gave a slight shake of her head, trying to make the pieces fall into place. "The last I heard, they were going to try bringing her out of her induced coma today."

Margie clasped her hands together and bowed her head. "Father God, please heal our precious girl." She looked back up at Debbie. "Are you a pray-er, Debbie?"

"Definitely. I hurt for those who don't have the hope only the Lord can bring." She waited a beat and then added, "I'm so sorry for your family. Ashling is truly one of the sweetest girls I have ever known. And so gifted. How many people her age start their own company and make a go of it?"

"We are proud of her. I can't help but wonder what she was doing driving around so early in the morning."

"Colleen didn't know?"

"Not that she told me. But then, our children do have a tendency to shelter us from unpleasantness." She gave a soft smile. "Anyway, we will wait for a good report. Now tell me about yourself and everything else that's happening in Dennison. One of my life regrets is losing touch with so many people who were important to me. My husband and I used to get back there at least once a year. It's so close, but life just interfered, you know? And now I can't see, hear, write, or type like I once could, so communication has gotten difficult. But enough about me. I want to hear about you."

"What would you like to know?"

"Give me your life story in a nutshell." She grinned at Debbie's stunned reaction. "It's something I say to every new resident here. At my age, I might not have time for the long version." She laughed.

"Well, I was born and raised in Dennison. My parents, Vance and Becca, are—"

"Vance Albright! I've met him. Sorry to interrupt. Like I said, life is short." Her eyes gleamed. "Jesse, my husband, golfed with him years ago. Some kind of fundraiser, I think. And wasn't he the head honcho at Good Shepherd?"

"Yes. You do keep tabs on things. My dad is retired now but still golfing. My mom works part time as a receptionist. I had a pretty unremarkable childhood, which is a good thing these days, I guess. I got engaged while I was in college, but my fiancé was killed in Afghanistan." She was surprised how easily and unemotionally she was able to convey that fact.

"I'm so sorry. War is awful."

"It is."

"I read about the café. Thanks to this." She lifted something that hung on a chain around her neck. The object had been hidden under a crocheted lap blanket. A magnifying glass. "I'm so thrilled for you and for the town. Back when they did all the renovations on the depot, Ray kept us updated. I just hate to see places that played such a vital role in our country's history torn down or fall down. Ray says you're compiling Christmas stories about the depot."

"Yes. Like the buildings, they need to be saved for future generations."

"Well, I've got a book's worth of stories, but I'm guessing I should lead with the most important one. Ray said he told you about how Jesse proposed to me."

"He did, but I'd love to hear more details. Would you mind if I record you?"

"Go right ahead."

"Thank you." She thought about telling Margie what she already knew, but that would involve mentioning the bench. Better to let her do that. She positioned the recorder on the small end table next to Margie.

"Jesse and I grew up together. He was my brother's best friend, and his sister Andrea was mine. The boys were two years older, so in high school we each had our own groups of friends, but I spent a lot of time at Andrea's. I had a secret crush on Jesse from the time I was thirteen, but I managed to keep it to myself until one night when I slept over and I said his name in my sleep." Margie laughed like a schoolgirl, covering her lips with her fingertips. "I was sixteen at the time, and from that moment on, Andrea did everything in her power to get us together. When their father got a job here in Ravenna, I thought I'd lost all hope of ever getting Jesse to look at me as more than his sister's tagalong friend, but then, in 1941, we were all at Kent State together. In August of '42, Jesse finally asked me out, but he'd already enlisted, so we only had one date. I didn't see him again until Christmas, when he was on a train that stopped in Dennison. He was headed to New York and shipping out in days."

Debbie thought back to what Madeline had said about that meeting. When she'd seen them together, Margie had run to him, but he'd pushed her away. Madeline thought they were arguing, and when the train had left, she'd seen Margie reading a note. Would Margie tell her any of that?

"We only had a few minutes together." The emotions playing across her face said she was reliving the moment. Debbie held her breath. "But then we started writing. In one of my letters, I told him about a bunch of soldiers who piled pyramid-style on an old rickety bench outside the depot to pose for a picture, and the bench collapsed. It was beyond repair, and I mentioned to Jesse that as soon as the war was over, I was going to ask my father to build one that would last. I suppose you know my father owned the furniture factory in town."

Debbie nodded. At that moment, Calista walked in, carrying two to-go cups. Since Debbie faced the door and Margie didn't, Calista was able to nod at the framed citation hanging on the wall and arch one eyebrow.

When Margie turned her head, Debbie gave a slight shrug, body language for "I don't know, but I hope we'll get around to that."

"Do you want anything from the cabinet, Margie? Photo albums or letters or anything?"

"Not at the moment. I'll tell Debbie where they are if we need them. Thank you very much for the drinks."

When the door closed behind Calista, Margie held the covered cup close to her nose and breathed deeply. "Thank the good Lord that even though most of my senses are getting fuzzy, I can still smell. Now, where were we? Oh, yes. Unbeknownst to me, when Jesse came home on leave the following December, the moment his feet touched US soil, he found a pay phone and called my father and asked for his blessing to propose to me. When he got my dad's approval, he asked him to make a bench for the depot and add a personalized touch to it."

Debbie sat up straight. "The heart and your initials. Your father did that?"

"Sure did."

"But I heard it came on the train."

"That was all my father's idea. He had quite the flair for the dramatic and wanted this to be a big thing. Nowadays young people do all sorts of crazy things for proposals, but it wasn't common then. My father was ahead of his time. He made the bench in record time then drove it to Pittsburgh, put it on the train Jesse was on, and had it sent right back here. I thought Jesse was coming in the next day, so when Andrea came to visit and hauled me out in front of the depot to watch the next train coming in, even though it was freezing out and I needed to be inside handing out doughnuts, I should have been suspicious. When the men brought this big, beautiful bench off the train and I saw the initials, I just kind of collapsed. A second later, Jesse jumped off the train and proposed."

Tears glinted in her eyes. "We were married five days later. Friends brought poinsettias to decorate the church, and I wore my mother's wedding dress. We got married in the evening, and the church was aglow with candlelight. It turned out more beautiful than if I'd planned it for months. Can you imagine planning a wedding that fast?"

She could. When Reed had asked her to marry him in a year, her answer hadn't been "Yes." It had been "Yes, but why don't we get married now, before you leave?" In the seconds it took him to answer, she'd already decided they could get married in two days, which would give them two days together as husband and wife. She would buy a secondhand dress and ask the women of the church to fix a simple meal. They would spend their two-day honeymoon at her grandparent's cabin on Tappan Lake.

She'd seen a moment of weakening in his eyes, but then he'd said, "I want you to have the wedding of your dreams. I don't want to start our life together with something rushed. If I get back before December, we can always move the date up, but planning a wedding will give you something positive to focus on while I'm gone."

And she had. Until Betsy had called, sobbing too hard to talk. Debbie gave herself a mental shake. This moment was not about her. "What a beautiful story."

"It is. And it's still going. We just celebrated our eightieth anniversary. We had a wonderful party. My son, Quinn, and my other daughter, Annie, were able to come, and most of the grandchildren and great-grandchildren. We missed Colleen and Ashling, of course."

"Happy anniversary." Debbie picked up her purse. "My friend Janet found something of yours this week." She pulled out the brown envelope.

Margie's hand flew to her mouth as she reached out to take it. "Is this…? Oh." The tears that had shimmered in her eyes moments ago now spilled over her lashes. "I've wondered what happened to this." She pressed it close. "It was at the depot?"

Debbie nodded.

"Jesse thought I was silly when I said I wished I still had this. My children put all of our old home movies on DVDs, but this...it was his first communication with me after..." She reached for a tissue and wiped her eyes. "Thank you. This is a true treasure." And then her smile faded. "I suppose you listened to it."

Heat crept up Debbie's neck. She hadn't thought they'd done anything wrong by playing the record, but now, seeing the envelope clutched in Margie's hand, she felt embarrassed, like she and Janet had deliberately invaded her privacy. "We did." A handful of excuses flooded her mind, but they all seemed weak.

Margie nodded but didn't say a word. Her gaze drifted to the window.

As much as Debbie wanted to pry and prod, she knew she couldn't. It was as if an invisible wall had gone up between them. Somewhere in the background a clock ticked. "I suppose you want to know what it was all about."

"I..." This was not what she'd expected. "Of course, I'm curious. Especially since I've heard rumors that you and your friend did something heroic to help the war effort."

Another long pause. "That was another Christmas memory. Are you wanting to put it in your booklet?"

"Only if you want me to. Or maybe it deserves a book of its own." She said it with a smile and was surprised when Margie offered one in return.

"Maybe it does. And maybe it's time." She closed her eyes for a moment, and Debbie tried to tamp down the adrenaline rush that made her want to jump out of her chair. "At first, we were ordered not to talk about it for security reasons. But now, there's probably no one left whose life would be affected. And maybe there's something in our story that can benefit—"

A soft knock at the door interrupted Margie. "Come in."

"Therapy in five minutes, Margie." The young woman in Santa Claus scrubs and dazzling earrings shaped like Christmas tree bulbs projected her voice across the room.

"Oh, fiddledeedee. I forgot about that. Ever since I broke my hip, they keep wanting to bend and twist me in all sorts of unnatural positions." She looked longingly at her cappuccino. "You're on your way to Cleveland?"

"Yes."

"Could you possibly stop by on your way back?"

Debbie sighed. "Unfortunately, I'll have two other people with me, so I can't."

"Hmm." Margie held her cup in both hands and tapped the side with one index finger. "I don't know why I'm doing this, but… I can trust you, can't I? Ray seems to think I can, and I guess that's good enough for me. If you promise me not to share this with anyone whose motives might be different than yours and to use discretion when it comes to more personal things…" Her finger stopped its staccato beat, and she looked as though she might be having second thoughts.

Then she nodded. "I will entrust my journal to you. It won't answer all of your questions. We'll have to talk again after you read it, but it's a start. I've never shown it to anyone, and lately I've been wondering if I should destroy it or give it to someone who would handle our story wisely. I do believe, Miss Albright, that you are the answer to my prayers."

CHAPTER NINETEEN

It took almost more willpower than Debbie possessed to start the car and keep driving the rest of the way to Cleveland when all she wanted to do was open the journal and start reading.

The nine-by-twelve red book sat on the passenger seat. At least a dozen paperclips ran like musical notes on a staff when she looked at it from the top. Likely holding newspaper clippings. Maybe letters or photographs. She'd opened it when she got in the car, just to see the penmanship. Pretty and neat, Margie McGarry's perfectly slanted writing reminded her of her third-grade teacher's. Margie had suggested she start reading on December 7, 1941. There she'd find a first-person account of the moment the world heard that the Japanese had bombed Pearl Harbor.

Her fingers crept across the console the same way they would have if a bag of caramel corn or Janet's chocolate chip cookies called to her from the next seat. She ran her fingertips across the cover, imagining nineteen-year-old Margie opening it to write the devastating news. The announcement that would change everything.

Suddenly, words seemed to come from somewhere outside of her mind, and somehow, she knew they didn't apply only to Margie. *And we know that in all things God works for the good of those who love him, who have been called according to his purpose.* Was Romans

8:28, the verse that seemed to flow out of her train of thought, true for everyone? What about for her? Reed's death was tragic. Had God worked anything for good because of that loss?

The answer came quickly. Yes. It had strengthened and deepened her dependence on Him. Though she'd had days of anger, of questioning God, she'd never felt His presence and comfort more than in the first few weeks following the devastating news. And it had deepened bonds. Her parents had hardly left her side for days. They'd let her sob or yell or curl in a fetal position, and then, after weeks of that, they'd gently encouraged her to open her eyes to the color and music and needs of others who still existed in her world.

"Thank You." She whispered the words as she took the exit to Hopkins International and followed the blue signs that led her to the parking lot. She'd have almost an hour to read. She shut off the car, pushed her chair back, and took a sip of the now cool cappuccino. Still sweet and delicious. She smiled as she remembered Margie's longing glance at her own cup, and how she'd comically blown it a kiss as she'd been wheeled to therapy. There was a strength and depth to the woman Debbie wanted to know more about. Despite her many struggles, Margie still found joy in little things.

Before opening the journal, Debbie thought back on what she'd learned about the bench. Even though they might never recover it, knowing its origin changed something in her mind. There was a strange kind of comfort in knowing the life story of the inanimate object that had been the stage to so many tender moments throughout decades.

She picked up the book, set it on her lap, and opened the front cover. The pages were pale green. A short line at the top right provided room for a date. The first one was September 10, 1938. She flipped to the last entry. New Year's Eve, 1943. She'd intended to start at Pearl Harbor like Margie had suggested, but she needed context. What was Margie like as a carefree college student before the war? How would it compare to her own life before 9/11? As she leafed through pages filled with words like "party," "study group," and "youth group meeting," her phone rang. Was Janet just checking in to see if she'd arrived?

"Hi. I made it, Mom." It was a running joke between them starting about three months after Reed died, at a time when Debbie was starting to heal and feeling a bit smothered by the many mother figures hovering around her. Smothered but immensely grateful.

"Good. I want to hear all about Margie, but first I have news. Brenda just called. She's at the hospital with Colleen. They're bringing Ashling out of her coma. I'm not sure how they go about it, but they started about an hour ago, and things look good so far. No more swelling on her brain."

"That's wonderful news. And on that subject, I have some news. Are you ready for this? Ashling is Jesse and Margie's great-granddaughter."

"What?"

"Yep. I almost fell off my chair. This isn't a coincidence." She glanced at the clock. Janet was likely home by now. "Do you have a minute?"

"All the time in the world for this story."

Debbie told her about Jesse calling Margie's father and how he made the bench and then put it on the train.

"I love this! Wouldn't that be fun to act out?"

"With the right people maybe. Anyway, Margie was good friends with all the Bench Bandits. She must be involved."

"Did she say anything about it going missing?"

"No. And I didn't bring it up, because Ray said he was afraid it would upset her. Now I'm thinking he didn't want me to talk about it because she might leak something about what they did with it."

"Maybe we shouldn't be messin' with this gang, sista." Janet's 1920's thug voice was Oscar-worthy.

"We may be dealing with a much more extensive underground senior network than we can handle." Debbie smiled as she pictured literal underground tunnels connecting senior living centers across the country. "Dis ting is biggah dan da bot' of us, Blondie."

In the car, waiting to hear Betsy's plane had landed, Debbie turned up the heat and once again opened Margie's journal, written more than eighty years ago. She started on the first page with the words, *This is absolutely dreadful. Dutch and Jesse have been gone for two weeks, and life in Dennison has lost its sparkle. 73 long, lonely, boring days stretch ahead until they'll be home for Thanksgiving. How will Andrea and I ever survive this tedious life?*

Debbie shook her head. "Oh, friend, I sure hope you enjoyed the next three years. I'm guessing you longed for a tedious life by 1942."

Page after page was filled with chatter about school and boys and fashion and movies. *Fantasia, Pinocchio, The Philadelphia Story, His Girl Friday, The Shop Around the Corner.* She'd seen almost every film Margie and Andrea had gone to. But seeing them

on the big screen for the first time, when the actors were still alive…
Once again, she wished for a time machine.

The next big crisis in Margie's young life occurred in the fall of
1940. Jesse and Andrea's father was assigned to oversee operations
of a new military installation in Ravenna. *Andrea is moving!* the
entry read. *This is absolutely the worst day of my life.* The bright blue
ink was smeared, making some of it hard to read.

Over the next few months, most journal entries were weekly,
beginning with, *Got a letter from Andrea today.* And then, in August
of 1941, Margie's world brightened again. She and Andrea would be
roommates at Kent State, sharing a dorm room with two other girls.
And they'd have a whole year of *a little studying and tons of fun with
Jesse and Dutch.* Debbie felt a pinch of sadness, knowing the pall
that would soon overshadow those starry-eyed plans.

September of 1941 began many short entries, mostly about Jesse.
The way he smiled at me today made me forget how to breathe.

*The man is infuriating! I swear he hasn't noticed one iota of
change in me since I was twelve.*

*I saw Jesse talking to a girl who looked like she just walked off a
Breck shampoo ad. Who am I, a lowly freshman, to think I can capture his eye?*

*Andrea came up with a plan. She thinks I should start flirting
with Barry. But that would be dishonest, wouldn't it? Barry
Cunningham is nice enough, but to cozy up to him just to make Jesse
jealous seems wrong. I don't think I can do it.*

When Debbie was a page away from December, she stopped,
took another long drink of cappuccino, and closed her eyes for a
moment, remembering her own world before everything changed.

She and Reed would meet to study together in the library or the student union and then go out for coffee. And talk. Though she missed his words of affection and his arms around her, it was the talking she missed most of all. Or maybe it was the listening.

He's interesting and funny and a great listener. Her own words about Greg came back to her. It was true. And another reminder that she couldn't keep living in the past.

As that thought resonated, her phone dinged with a text from Betsy. AT BAGGAGE CLAIM.

Strange timing that her thoughts about moving on were interrupted by someone who was here in Ohio for the express purpose of reliving the past. She put the car in gear and whispered a prayer for strength. "Let me honor Betsy, and Reed's memory, while still keeping my eyes focused on the future You have prepared for me."

Tanned and toned, Betsy looked like a completely different person than she had been the last time they'd met. She hoisted her largest bag into the back of the car before Debbie could grab it then wrapped her in an enthusiastic embrace. "It's so good to be with you. We're going to have fun."

So maybe they were on the same page after all. Maybe this would be a joyful time of reminiscing and honoring Reed's memory instead of a somber walk down memory lane. "Yes, we are. Hotel first?"

"Yes, please. And then, if you're okay with it, I made reservations at the hotel restaurant."

How could it not be okay with her? The contemporary eating establishment was what she supposed would be called understated. Sleek lines, a color pallet of brown, tan, and white. No tablecloths.

The chairs were dark brown and chrome. Casual. But with a seasonal international menu that might include delicacies like Chilean sea bass, cassoulet, salmon and dill pie, shrimp Mozambique, vanilla flan, or Sicilian cookies with honey sorbet, the smells alone wrapped around guests like a hug from home. "I am more than okay with that." Her stomach rumbled, and they both laughed. So far, this trip was starting out so much lighter than she'd imagined.

As she pulled onto I-71, Betsy said, "I just read that the bench out in front of the depot was stolen."

"It's on the news?"

"I have alerts on my phone for all sorts of things. Dennison is one of them. While I was waiting to board this morning, I got an alert for a travel blog. It said the bench just disappeared and no one knows how or why. Is that true?"

"Yes." She wouldn't share what they'd seen on the security footage. "A week ago today, I came to work before it was light out, and the bench was gone. I think we've talked to everyone in town who might have had a reason to have it moved, but no one seems to know anything." It wasn't the full story, but it was enough for now.

"That's so sad. I love looking at all the family Christmas pictures people post online. And it has special meaning to you."

Debbie nodded. "There are hundreds of names and dates on it. I've even seen people lying down to carve something beneath the seat. I would guess just about every family in town has put their mark on that bench, and then you consider all the tourists over so many years...it's irreplaceable."

It was the first time that word had come to mind, but it was true.

She thought for a moment about telling Betsy about the journal, now tucked away in a plastic bag in the tote in the back seat that held her ugly Christmas sweater, white elephant gift, and seven-layer bars. Margie's request that she only share it with like-minded people flashed in her mind. Betsy had a big heart, but her marriage had ended in divorce about ten years ago and she still harbored a good deal of bitterness, at least she had the last time they'd had a soul-deep talk. How would she handle hearing a tender love story about a relationship that had lasted more than eight decades?

Until Debbie knew more, she'd keep it to herself.

December 18, 1942

The concentration on Andrea's face as she leaned close to the phonograph on her desk almost made Margie laugh. If there wasn't so much at stake, she might have. When Andrea lifted the needle off the record, the look stayed in place. "Trojan Horse. So Jonathan Goldman is not working alone."

Margie nodded. "That's what I thought too."

"I wonder if Jesse is telling us that this is much, much bigger than we imagined? There were forty soldiers in the wooden horse with Odysseus."

"Could be. Jonathan talks a lot about his adventures, all here in the States, but there's no doubt he's German. He's clearly worked hard to cover it up, but there were a few words where his Ws came out like Vs. And there's that picture Laverne said was taken in Milwaukee. I've been to Milwaukee many times, and I don't believe a word of it."

Andrea pushed her bangs out of her face. "He sure has my dad fooled. And poor Laverne."

Margie scooted back against the headboard of Andrea's bed. "I feel sorry for her. I don't think she has any idea what he's doing."

"I know. I think he's using her. She's just part of his ruse, naive enough for whatever his evil schemes are."

"If Jonathan is what we think he is, one way or another, she's going to get hurt." The next thought that struck made Margie's blood run cold. "Would he hurt her? Physically, I mean?"

Andrea's lips parted. Clearly, she hadn't considered that possibility. "I suppose it depends on what she knows. I don't believe she's part of whatever the Trojan Horse is, but she's likely overheard or seen things he wouldn't want her repeating."

"We'll have to look out for anything concerning her tonight."

Andrea rubbed her arms as if she'd gotten a sudden chill. "Is what we're going to do crazy?"

"Probably crazy. Definitely illegal. But this is exactly what we'd be doing if we officially worked for the government."

"True."

"No second thoughts about talking to your father or someone higher up?"

The shake of Andrea's head was decisive. "If I knew for sure who I could trust, I would." Her shoulders rose and fell, and she looked away. "I'm not even a hundred percent sure my father is on the right side."

"Andrea! You're serious?"

"I don't know. I feel awful for thinking it, but we need to face the facts. He has eyes on top-secret information about our latest weapons and where they're being sent, and..." Her sigh filled the room. "He gave my mom a ring with a huge ruby in it for her last birthday. Now, when we're all supposed to be tightening our belts, he's spending money on frivolous things? Why? How?" Her eyes shimmered with tears. "What if my father is selling information to the Nazis?"

Margie reached out and laid her hand on Andrea's arm. "That's only speculation. It's also possible he is simply as naive and charmed by Jonathan as Laverne is."

A slight smile teased Andrea's lips as she tugged a handkerchief out of her pocket. "That's a nice way of telling me I have an overactive imagination."

"In this case, it would be a good thing. Now, I told you I had two things to show you."

"Yes, I forgot. What did you bring?"

Margie leaned forward and picked up her purse from the end of the bed. With what she hoped was a look of mystery on her face, she pulled out an envelope.

Andrea stared at the return address. "Jesse! He sent you two things this week and nothing for me?"

"This is for both of us, but I can't understand half of it. I need you to break the code."

CHAPTER TWENTY

*A*nother unrushed morning. It was after eight o'clock, yet Debbie sat in bed, propped up on a cloud of pillows in an elegant room on the fifth floor of their lovely hotel, reading today's entry from the devotional she'd brought along. Betsy was still sleeping, so she read by the glow of her phone's flashlight.

If ever she needed assurance that God knew her thoughts before they formed in her brain, the words in front of her put all doubt to rest.

The devotion started with a verse from the forty-third chapter of the Book of Isaiah. *"Forget the former things; do not dwell on the past. See, I am doing a new thing! Now it springs up; do you not perceive it? I am making a way in the wilderness and streams in the wasteland."*

She closed her eyes. *Lord, if You're doing a new thing in my life, I'm ready. I think.* Would she be more ready by the end of the weekend? Or less? Could she revisit memory-laden spots and simply be grateful for what she once had? Could she spend time with old friends who had made tons of shared memories without her in the past year and be thankful she was still included, if only occasionally?

Needing something to anchor her thoughts to home, she texted Rachel. Everything going okay?

After a few minutes, she received a long response, peppered with exclamation points.

EVERYTHING IS WONDERFUL! I STILL HAVE TO PINCH MYSELF TO BELIEVE THIS IS REAL. FOUR DAYS AGO, WE WERE LIVING IN A SHELTER WITH FIFTY OTHER WOMEN AND CHILDREN. SUSANNAH AND I TOOK A WALK YESTERDAY AFTERNOON. I LOVE YOUR LITTLE TOWN! WE MIGHT STAY HERE! WE STOPPED IN AT YOUR CAFÉ. IT'S ADORABLE, AND YOU WERE RIGHT ABOUT JANET. SHE WELCOMED US LIKE WE WERE OLD FRIENDS—JUST LIKE YOU DID. AND THOSE CINNAMON ROLLS! OH MY. IT MIGHT BE A BLESSING IN DISGUISE THAT WE LOST MOST OF OUR CLOTHES, BECAUSE WE JUST MAY NEED TO BUY BIGGER SIZES!

SUSANNAH WAS FASCINATED BY THE MUSEUM. I HEARD PEOPLE TALKING ABOUT THE MISSING DEPOT BENCH. WHAT A STRANGE THING FOR SOMEONE TO TAKE. WE HAD SOMETHING SIMILAR HAPPEN BACK HOME WHEN A BUST OF ROBERT CAVELIER DE LA SALLE DISAPPEARED FROM THE LIBRARY LAWN. IT TURNED OUT TO BE A PRANK BY A FRATERNITY. IT SHOWED UP A FEW DAYS LATER IN FRONT OF A RIVAL FRAT HOUSE, WITH A BABY BONNET AND PACIFIER! IT WAS PUT BACK IN PLACE AND THEN GOT TAKEN AND DRESSED UP THREE MORE TIMES BEFORE THE LIBRARY FOUND A PLACE FOR IT INSIDE. GOODNESS, I'M RAMBLING. ALL THIS TO SAY, YES, EVERYTHING IS WONDERFUL AND WE CANNOT THANK YOU ENOUGH. YOUR HOME (AND TOWN) IS SUCH A HAVEN OF PEACE...THE PERFECT ENVIRONMENT FOR US TO START FRESH. THANK YOU.

Debbie pondered the last sentence. *Your home (and town) is such a haven of peace...the perfect environment for us to start fresh.* It was true. Old friends had enfolded her back into the circle. It was good to be close to her parents. Opening the café was just the fresh start she'd needed. But continuing her tradition of spending half of December reflecting on all she had lost was taking a step backward. Maybe she would always, for the rest of her life, think about Reed on the anniversaries of their engagement and his death, but she needed to change the way she thought about him. She had been loved by a man who cherished her. Many women never got to experience that. It was something to be deeply grateful for. From now on she needed to face those dates with thankfulness. She listened to Betsy's quiet breathing. Would she be open to the idea for herself?

She wrote a short response to Rachel then pushed the button on the side of her phone, but just before the screen went dark, she caught a single word in Rachel's text. *Rival.* Debbie had latched on to the idea of the Silver Sneakers gang being their bench bandits, hiring Ashling to move it…someplace. That theory had eclipsed their thoughts about rivals for the *Ohio Heritage* contest. She pushed the button again and went to her search engine to find information about the contest. She scrolled through the list of articles, and one caught her attention with the heading *It's Going to Be a Hard Choice, Folks.* After praising the editors of the magazine for their choices, the author applauded each town for its unique Christmas spirit.

Clifton – Specifically, the Clifton Mill. Every year they string four million *lights along the exterior of the historic mill, along the gorge and riverbanks, and in the surrounding trees and bridges. Mind-blowing, people! And if that's not enough Christmas spirit, there's also a Santa museum, a vintage toy collection, and a crazy cool display of miniature villages.*

Lebanon – The Annual Lebanon Horse Drawn Carriage Parade and Festival is fabulous. Go there. Seriously.

Cambridge – The historic downtown becomes "Christmas in the Dickens Victorian Village" with all the buildings decked out in full Victorian holiday splendor from November to December. Breathtaking.

Dennison – Ride the Dennison Christmas Train! Get on the vintage train and ride through the (hopefully) snow-covered countryside while you nosh on cocoa and cookies and elves entertain you. Bring the fam and have your pic taken on the iconic depot bench that's been carved with names and dates going back to WWII. Seriously, don't miss this. My family does it every year. Way cool.

Coshocton – Take the Christmas tour in Historic Roscoe Village and enjoy a variety of family-friendly holiday activities, including holiday shopping and A Roscoe Christmas tour. The Christmas Candle Lighting Ceremony on December 2 and 9 begins at 6 p.m. at the base of the thirty-five-foot tree. A heartwarming experience.

The comments following were, as was often the case, more interesting than the article itself. She stopped scrolling to read one from "ChristmasCrazy."

Seriously? This is even a contest? Everyone knows that Coshocton has the best Christmas tree, the best roasted chestnuts and hot cider, the best candle lighting, the best everything. The other towns are nice, but they don't begin to compare with what we have to offer at Christmas. Don't worry, Coshocton. We've got this.

Wasn't it a conflict of interest that Coshocton, the home of *Ohio Heritage*, was even allowed in the competition? Since most commentors used real names, Debbie couldn't help but wonder about ChristmasCrazy. Was he or she a regular reader, or someone connected with the magazine? She almost laughed out loud at the thought of Terrance Aschauer, the oh-so-proper receptionist, secretly typing comments.

Whoever ChristmasCrazy was, did he have a following? Could he have influenced the vote? She copied the link and sent it to Janet, along with a few of the thoughts swirling through her head, then picked up Margie's journal. She'd just opened to December 7, 1941, once again, when Janet answered her message: CAN YOU TALK?

NOT AT THE MOMENT. BETSY IS SLEEPING. THOUGHTS?

ONLY MORE QUESTIONS. I KNOW SOME PEOPLE IN COSHOCTON, AND IAN HAS A FRIEND FROM THE POLICE ACADEMY IN CAMBRIDGE. I'M GOING TO ASK HIM IF HE CAN TALK TO THE DEPARTMENTS IN THOSE TOWNS AND ASK THEM TO KEEP A LOOKOUT FOR THE BENCH. ASHLING WOULDN'T HAVE HAD TIME TO TAKE IT FAR BEFORE HER ACCIDENT, BUT SHE WASN'T IN HER OWN TRUCK, SO WHO KNOWS?

I HOPE IAN AGREES. HOW'S BUSINESS?

HOPPING. WEIRD YOU'RE NOT HERE. PAULETTE IS AMAZING. SHE'LL MAKE SOMEBODY A GREAT M-I-L SOMEDAY.

This last comment was followed by a wink emoji.

Debbie stifled a laugh and replied with GET BACK TO WORK then picked up the journal. She read the first entry.

I have never been so afraid in all my life. Japan has attacked the US! Everyone says we will be at war in a matter of hours. We all gathered around radios this afternoon as word spread. It started like a normal day. Andrea and I going to church with Dutch and Jesse followed by lunch at the Hollenden for Dutch's birthday. We first heard the news on the radio in the cab on our way back to campus. The first thing Dutch and Jesse said was—

Betsy yawned and stretched and sat up. Before Debbie had a chance to say good morning, Betsy said, "I have something to tell you. I thought maybe I should wait until after this week, but I just can't keep it to myself." She threw the covers off and swung her legs over the side of the bed. A smile, the kind Debbie hadn't seen in decades, spread across her face. "I met someone. And he asked me to marry him."

I met someone. While Betsy showered, the words looped through Debbie's mind. She'd thought about telling Betsy about Greg during dinner, but it had just seemed all wrong. How could she tell the woman who had almost become her mother-in-law that she was interested in someone else? But now…

Genuinely thrilled for Betsy, Debbie had jumped up and hugged her then listened to her description of the music store owner she'd met in Florida. A Christian man with two daughters and four grandchildren who'd lost his wife to cancer three years ago, he sounded like the perfect match. Betsy would finally have the grandchildren Debbie hadn't had the chance to give her. Surprisingly, the thought didn't hurt as much as it might have at one time.

When Betsy came out of the bathroom, wearing a bright red blouse over black pants and brighter makeup than usual, Debbie said, "I have something to tell you too." She took a deep breath. "I've met someone. We're not actually dating yet, but…"

Betsy's expression froze for just a fraction of a breath. Tears filled her eyes, and Debbie's stomach clenched. In the next moment, Betsy pressed a hand to her chest and shouted, "Praise God!"

Debbie, standing in front of the mirror and fastening an earring, stepped back in surprise and dropped the earring. "Like I said, we're not actually dating yet, but there's definitely something happening. He's the man I hired to put guest rooms in the base—"

Engulfed in a hug, she couldn't finish her explanation.

"I'm just so, so happy for you. I'll admit, it took me about ten years before I could start asking the Lord to send you someone to love, but it's been a fervent prayer ever since." Betsy sat on the end of her bed. "Tell me all about him."

Debbie blinked back tears. This was not the reaction she'd expected. "He's tall, blue eyes, very handsome. He's a contractor, and the president of the Dennison Chamber of Commerce. He has two sons. Jaxon is a freshman in high school, and Julian is in seventh grade. They…" She stopped as tears began coursing down Betsy's face. Maybe this was too much for her to handle. "I'm sorry. I—"

"Children," Betsy said through tears, a smile shimmering in her eyes. "God has put children in your life."

Debbie nodded. "I don't know what the future holds for us, but it means so much to have your blessing."

Betsy blew her nose and smiled. "This week, let's not let this be a sad time. Let's focus on all of the good times."

Goose bumps shimmied up Debbie's spine. "I couldn't agree more." She stepped to her bed and picked up her devotional book. After opening to the page she'd read earlier, she handed it to Betsy and pointed at the verse. Betsy read it out loud. "'Forget the former things; do not dwell on the past. See, I am doing a new thing! Now it springs up; do you not perceive it? I am making a way in the wilderness and streams in the wasteland.'" She swiped at her damp cheek. "I can't help but believe that thousands of years ago when God inspired Isaiah to write this, he knew that someday there would be two women who had shared pain in their pasts who would need these exact words at just the right time."

Debbie acknowledged this with a smile. "Let's go have a fantastic breakfast and start focusing on all the good times in the past and the ones yet to come."

Betsy picked up her jacket and purse. "I'm ready!" She said it with conviction and joy in her voice.

Not wanting to take a chance on Margie's journal sliding off the bed when housekeeping came in to straighten, Debbie picked it up to put it in her overnight bag. As she turned, something fluttered onto the bed. A piece of folded paper torn from a small notepad. Before she opened it, she saw a date penciled on the back. *December 1, 1942.* A single sentence was written on the inside.

Tell Father not to give the gold ring from David King's friend for Christmas Eve. The man can't be trusted.

December 18, 1942

Margie studied Andrea's face as she read the short letter from Jesse out loud. The first three paragraphs talked about his two days in New York City before shipping out. It read like a travel brochure, with nothing personal. When she got to the third paragraph, a smile broke across her face. "See that little dot?"

Margie leaned closer and squinted at a tiny dot of ink, barely noticeable, the kind of mark a person might make if hesitating on the next word. She turned to Margie with a questioning look.

"That's our sign. That's where the code starts." She ran her fingertip along the words, silently forming them with her lips.

I hope you'll make cranbarry pie for my good friend very soon. He has a photograph sent in May and has proof the man standing directly above Father is not who we thought he is. Father will want to know that and will want to tell Israel.

"I think I figured out the first part," Margie said. "He didn't accidentally misspell cranberry, did he?"

Andrea smiled. "You're catching on. So, Barry has proof of...what? The man standing directly above Father..."

"His superior? Who is your dad's boss?"

"Captain Brooks." Andrea's eyes shot wide. "He came to Ravenna in May. And above Brooks is Major Sterling. Major Jacob Sterling."

"Israel!" Margie jumped out of her seat. "In Genesis, God tells Jacob he is going to be called Israel! So Barry has proof that Brooks can't be trusted, but Sterling can?"

"I think that's it." Andrea stood. "I'm going to call Barry and invite him over for a piece of pie tomorrow night."

CHAPTER TWENTY-ONE

By four o'clock, Debbie was more tired than she'd been in a long time, but it was a good tired. They'd hit all the places Betsy had suggested, starting with the Rock & Roll Hall of Fame, where they'd taken silly selfies. Instead of a sit-down lunch, they'd opted to graze their way through West Side Market, splitting a pastrami sandwich then moving on to Hungarian cheese biscuits, orange-pineapple smoothies, and finally indulging in elaborately decorated Christmas cookies. Then they'd strolled through the art museum. In each place, they talked about Reed's practical jokes and his uncanny knack for buying the perfect gift. They'd shed a few tears. And laughed.

As she drove into the hotel parking garage, Debbie tried explaining the good-tired feeling to Betsy. "It's like my emotions are finally in sync with my body."

"I get that." When Debbie parked the car, Betsy turned to face her. "After Reed died, and again when the tension in my marriage started increasing, I had a lot of sleepless nights. Little by little, God has been healing all the hurt. Today was another step in that process. We gave ourselves some closure, didn't we?"

"We did. I think we both just might be ready for something new."

"While you're at your party, I think I'm going to read and take a nap…and make a phone call." The blush pinking her cheeks made her look far younger than sixty-four.

In their room, Debbie touched up her hair and makeup, hung a plastic ornament from each ear, and changed into jeans and her ugly sweater. She'd bought it at an after-Christmas sale last year, and her initial audience had the right reaction. Betsy burst out laughing as Debbie walked out of the bathroom and spread her arms wide. "You're a fireplace!" The sweater was red, printed to look like bricks. Gold lamé flames danced over her middle. But the best part was the "mantel." A strip of green garland wrapped in battery-operated lights ran from one wrist to the other, and all along it hung five-inch-long Christmas stockings.

"If there's a prize, I think you'll win," Betsy said.

"Not sure I want to. A few years ago, the prize was a burrito blanket. A big, round blanket that looked exactly like a burrito. Another time it was a box of *mis*fortune cookies." As Betsy laughed, Debbie gave her a one-armed hug, careful not to dislodge any stockings, and told her she'd be back by seven for their dinner reservation at the restaurant.

Stephanie's apartment was half an hour away, giving her some time to ponder the words on the slip of paper that had fallen out of Margie's journal. *Tell Father not to give the gold ring from David King's friend for Christmas Eve. The man can't be trusted.* Pushing it out of her mind all day had been difficult. If Ray hadn't told her that Margie couldn't hear well enough to talk on the phone, she would have called her. Was it a straightforward, though oddly worded, message? Who wrote it, and why did Margie save it? It wasn't in her handwriting.

When she parked in front of Stephanie's building, she grabbed the book and turned to the first paper clip, and then the second and third. An award ribbon, a photo, a newspaper clipping, and then she found what she was looking for. A letter from Jesse. The writing matched. That confirmed that the cryptic message about David King's friend had been written by Jesse.

Something Jesse had said in the Voice-O-Graph came back to her. *"Please share my letters with the one who knows the way we did things as kids. I don't dare communicate directly."* What did he mean by "the way we did things as kids"? Was there a hidden meaning in this? And then she remembered Madeline telling them about the first time she'd seen Margie and Jesse together. He'd just gotten off the train, and Margie had run toward him, reaching up for a hug, but he'd rebuffed her. *"When the train left, I saw her reading a note."*

Could this be the note? If Margie and Andrea were spies, the words could have relayed crucial information from Jesse to Margie. No, to Andrea, his sister. *"Tell Father..."*

Andrea and Jesse's family had moved to Ravenna before the US entered the war. Maybe a year before Pearl Harbor, if she remembered right. Their father was in charge of the munitions plant there. Debbie's heart did a hop-skip. A munitions plant would be a primary target.

Before getting out of the car, she took a moment to try to bring her thoughts back to the present. Some experts claimed that men had mental boxes they could crawl into and think about absolutely nothing. How she wished she could do that for the next three hours. And then she'd have twenty minutes to think again before dinner. With a deep breath, she gathered her things, entered the building, took the elevator, and walked into the party, her thoughts mirroring her costume, with sparks shooting in every direction.

Within sixty seconds, Debbie was smothered in a group hug that started with Stephanie and her sister Carrie then grew until it seemed she was cocooned by every person at the party. When the laughing horde finally peeled away, her emotions were in such turmoil she wasn't sure if she wanted to laugh or cry. Being at the center of so much affection, albeit silly, felt good. She'd missed this feeling of being part of a whole. While she was making new friends in Dennison and reconnecting with people she'd lost touch with, she didn't yet have *this*.

The next two hours were filled with catching up, exchanging cookies, deep discussions on what, exactly, constituted ugly when it came to sweaters, a wild gift exchange in which she ended up with a wall-mount singing fish, and sampling everything on Stephanie's overladen kitchen island. Carrie, who owned a catering company, had supplied the magazine-worthy spread of finger food. Little white cards lettered with calligraphy named each one. *Crostini Appetizer with Goat Cheese, Pomegranate, and Rosemary. Bacon-Wrapped Water Chestnuts. Smoked Salmon Bites. Stuffed Mushrooms. Cranberry-Brie Puffs.* Knowing she was only a couple of hours away from dinner, Debbie tried to control herself. But when Stephanie brought out a tray of chocolate-dipped cheesecake-on-a-stick, she gave up on self-control and simply enjoyed every bite.

"Coffee?"

Debbie looked up, and up, into a face she hadn't seen since Reed's funeral. "Nathan!" As tears sprang to her eyes, she held her dessert out of the way and threw one arm around him, careful not to jostle the coffee cups he held in each hand.

"Sorry I was late. It's so good to see you, Deb." His eyes searched hers.

"How did you…why are you here?" It sounded a bit rude, but he would understand. He'd been one of Reed's best friends but hadn't been part of this circle. The last she'd heard from him, he was still in the army, now with a desk job in Washington, DC.

"I've been…in touch with Stephanie since I got permanently stationed stateside." This big, strong marksman who'd done three tours in Afghanistan was blushing.

Once, before he and Reed had shipped out, the four of them had gone on a double date. She smiled at him. "In…touch?"

"Well, maybe a little more than that." He gestured to two empty chairs near the fireplace.

She nodded and followed him. A part of her was a tiny bit hurt that Stephanie hadn't shared this information. Another part knew why. Steph was protecting her. She took the mug Nathan handed her. "Tell me more."

"We've been texting for a while, and now that I'm home for two weeks, we're seeing each other as often as we can. That's all there is to tell. For now. So, tell me about you. I really like the pictures you post of the café. I want to come down and see it, and the museum. I've thought about contacting you. I've become a bit of a World War II geek since my grandpa died. We found his old army trunk in his basement. He must have come home from Italy in 1945 and never opened it again. Khakis, helmet, dress uniform, letters from home, photographs, even his shaving kit and toothpaste. K rations too. All in great condition. At least to look at. Not sure I'd try eating anything." He laughed. "I just found out from one of the letters I've been slowly reading that he stopped over in Dennison in 1942. The trunk is mine now, and I'd like to donate it. Would the museum be interested?"

Debbie's eyebrows crept up with each item he listed. "Interested? The museum director would be beyond ecstatic for something that well preserved." She could only imagine Kim's reaction to such a find. "1942..." She hadn't intended to say it out loud. Should she tell him what she'd discovered? Had God put Nathan Wade back in her life for just this reason? "Do you know anything about the army munitions plant in Ravenna during the war?"

"A bit. I toured it years ago. Why?"

"It's kind of a long story."

"I love long stories."

She glanced at her watch. "I need to leave in twenty minutes to meet Reed's mom. I'll try to make it short."

"Betsy's in town? I'd love to see her."

"Well, maybe we can arrange that."

"Great. Begin your long story. I'll watch the clock."

She started with the missing bench and told him everything, right up to the slip of paper falling out of Margie's journal.

"Wow. Fascinating. I know a guy who might be able to find out more details. So you think this Margie and her friend were spies?"

"I know they did something heroic and received a commendation from President Eisenhower. I don't know what they did. I'm hoping I'll learn something from the journals."

He pulled out his phone. "I'll text my buddy, and hopefully he can tell me something before you head home. Do you and Betsy have plans for breakfast?"

"We're in agreement that we want something delicious and not too early, but that's as far as we got in our planning."

"How about if Steph and I treat the two of you to a brunch buffet near the lake?" He named a pricey restaurant.

"That would be...extravagant."

"My pleasure. Let's say ten o'clock. That should give me time to learn something."

Debbie said her goodbyes, enjoyed being squished in another group hug, and left. In the car, she checked her phone. She'd missed a text from Janet. Ashling is awake, and things seem fine. She has an ulcer on her vocal cords from intubation, so doctors don't want her talking for at least 24 hours.

A second text was from Sonya at Good Shepherd. I don't know why I didn't think of this while you were here. A couple of weeks ago I overheard Eileen, Ray, and Madeline in Ray's room, talking about the bench in front of the depot. I was just outside the door with the med cart. When I walked in, they quickly changed the subject, but not before I heard Madeline say, "I'll take it."

December 19, 1942

Margie's gloved hand shook as she brought the key to the lock. She had knocked first, just to be sure. Ready with an excuse if Jonathan and Laverne had changed their plans, she almost blurted, "We saw Jonathan's car when we drove past," when the lock clicked.

The door opened silently. They entered, and Andrea shut it behind them.

"It's so dark," Andrea whispered.

"Flashlights." Margie pulled hers from the purse she'd slung across her chest.

In the glow of two bobbing lights, the apartment looked shrouded and eerie. Margie aimed her beam at the long, heavy drapes across the room. "I'm going to make sure the balcony door is unlocked." They'd planned their quick escape on the off chance they heard another key in the door. There had been two apartment keys on Jonathan's dresser. She'd taken the one that wasn't on the ring, but surely he'd noticed the other one was missing. She was surprised he hadn't changed the lock. But maybe he'd left it on purpose. Because he, or someone else, kept watch, waiting to catch a thief. She strode across the room, trying to shake fear with every stride. She unlocked the glass door and left the drapes parted just enough that they'd be able to find the opening in a hurry.

Andrea was already in the bedroom, searching drawers. The desk in the living room was Margie's to look through. If they found anything, they would take a photograph. She'd read enough crime novels to know that nothing they found could be used as evidence in court, but it could be used to prove to the army that Jonathan Goldman was up to no good.

In spite of little heat coming from the radiators, Margie felt perspiration trickling down her back after half an hour of searching. She'd searched every desk drawer, even running her hand underneath like she'd seen in a movie. Nothing incriminating. Pens, pencils, stationery, stamps, bills. She'd found a yearbook from Cleveland College and looked up Jonathan. He was there, in the class of '37. So that part of his story was true. Was this just a wild-goose chase, something conjured in Jesse's and Barry's minds?

No. Jesse was not prone to flights of fancy.

It was time to start thinking like a spy. She stood and turned slowly. If she wanted to hide something in a place no one would think to look... Could there be something taped under the kitchen sink? She checked but found nothing. She checked the almost bare cupboards, *inside an oatmeal box, and the bottom of the waste-basket. She went in the bathroom and lifted the lid off the tank. There were no pictures on the walls to look behind. Stopping in the bedroom doorway, she saw Andrea easing the back off the framed picture of Jonathan and his mother, lifting the glass gingerly with her cotton-gloved hand.*

Margie returned to the kitchen. The refrigerator? She stood in front of it, at eye level with the General Electric bracket. She tugged on the chrome handle, and the door opened with a squeak.

Laverne's comment about Jonathan's medicine cabinet held true for his refrigerator. A bottle of milk, a box of butter, an open can of Spam covered with waxed paper, and a block of cheese. Then she opened the small freezing compartment. An ice tray. And a carton of vanilla ice cream. She picked up the carton to look beneath it. It was far too light. She pulled it out and opened the flaps. No ice cream. But it wasn't empty. A wooden pencil box with a sliding lid, the kind she'd used in elementary school, sat inside.

And inside the pencil box was a folded map. A Pennsylvania Railroad map.

"Andrea!" she shouted in a stage whisper. "I found something."

Footsteps hurried toward her. "Me too!"

Andrea held a tiny roll of paper in the palm of her hand. "I found it in a chewing tobacco can in the toe of a shoe." She unrolled the paper with care, revealing two lines of numbers and letters.

12 24 11 P R

12 24 12 P SB

"December 24. That's easy. Eleven p.m.? What's the R..." She didn't need to finish.

"Ravenna." Andrea's voice was a ragged whisper. She took several shuddering breaths. "What does SB stand for?"

"Maybe this." Margie opened the map with trembling hands. A black line ran from St. Louis to Pittsburgh with shorter lines branching out from it, reminding her of a diagram of nerves she'd seen in a friend's anatomy book. A tiny circle of red was the only color on the page. It surrounded the town of Steubenville. Half an hour away by train, smack in the middle between Pittsburgh and Dennison.

"The Steubenville Bridge." Andrea breathed the words then reached out and braced herself with a hand on the wall. "Don't the...troop trains...cross...?"

All Margie could do was nod.

CHAPTER TWENTY-TWO

*O*s she and Betsy waited for Nathan and Steph on Sunday morning, Debbie sipped fresh-squeezed orange juice from a cobalt-blue glass and soaked in the panoramic view of Cleveland and sunlight glinting on Lake Erie.

This restaurant had been in operation for almost sixty years. She'd eaten there several times, but its unique architecture never failed to amaze her. Designed to resemble the hull of a cruise ship, the building nestled in a cliff overlooking the lake.

They'd arrived early to have time to case the buffet. "One must be strategic about these things," Betsy had declared with a pathetic British accent. They'd strolled past the salad bar with offerings of Caesar salad, antipasti, avocado toast, smoked trout, seaweed salad, fresh oysters, and artfully arranged mounds of fresh fruit. When they'd moved on to the labeled chafing dishes filled with beef medallions, Amish roasted chicken, salmon with lobster sauce, cheese blintzes, and prime rib, she'd said, "One must be careful not to indulge too heavily on appetizers and entrées and not leave room for waffles. And cheesecake."

"And crème brulée, bread pudding, chocolate mousse, chocolate-dipped strawberries…" Debbie's stomach had given an unladylike growl as she added to Betsy's list.

"Good morning!" Stephanie's cheerful greeting pulled her away from the sunlit skyline.

Debbie stood and hugged Nathan and then Steph. While she'd hoped for a few minutes alone with her old roommate to get the scoop on her and Nathan's relationship, what she most looked forward to, other than the incredible brunch, was finding out if Nathan had uncovered any details about Jesse's, Margie's, and Andrea's heroism.

Nathan, seeming to read her mind, said, "First things first. We load up our plates, and then I'll tell you what I know."

Getting in line behind Stephanie, Debbie couldn't help but think of when they'd done the same thing in the college cafeteria. "A little different fare than breakfast burritos and burgers."

Stephanie laughed. "Remember that mystery dish we avoided our whole freshman year?"

Debbie laughed with her. Both from small towns, neither of them had ever tasted Pad Thai before. Noodles with scrambled egg, peanuts, and grated carrots had looked too scary to try. "It's one of my favorites now."

With plates in both hands, they all settled at the table. "Shall I pray?" Nathan asked. When the three women nodded, he said a short prayer of gratitude for old friends reuniting and for "bountiful" food. After seeing the price of the brunch, Debbie offered up her own thanks for Nathan's generosity. The cost for one person could feed a table of four at the café.

Nathan took several bites followed by a swig of coffee. "Before I say anything… What I'm going to tell you is all I know. For now. My buddy's digging deeper, but it looks like a lot of the records have been redacted. So…here's what he found out." He drummed his fingers on the tablecloth and made eye contact with Betsy, then Steph, and finally Debbie. "Just before midnight on December 24, 1942, there was an explosion at the Ravenna Army Ammunitions Plant."

Even though he probably wouldn't have answers, Debbie couldn't refrain from voicing a few questions. "Was anyone killed? How much damage was done? Why were Margie and Andrea called heroes if they didn't stop it? Isn't there a statute of limitations on a lot of redacted documents? After eighty years, isn't there a chance we could—"

Nathan held up a hand. "I'm a step ahead of you." He picked up his phone and handed it to her. It was open to an article titled *Files on War Crimes*. She read the first line out loud.

"The US government has declassified more than 8.5 million pages of previously sealed World War II documents." She looked up. "So now all we have to do is sort through eight and a half million documents?"

Nathan laughed. "Yep. Easy-peasy."

Debbie hugged Janet and Ian's daughter on Sunday afternoon. As they stood in front of her dorm, Tiffany clung to her. Usually bubbly, the poor girl had dark circles under her eyes and looked like she hadn't slept in days. When she finally pulled back, she thanked Debbie again for coming to pick her up then said, "Hugging you feels like I'm already home."

"I wish you were coming home for a better reason, but it sounds like Ashling is going to make a full recovery," Debbie said. She'd gotten a text with the encouraging news from the church prayer chain coordinator that morning. "She's going to need her best buddy." Debbie hoped Tiffany wasn't going home to hear that her best friend was going to be arrested for theft.

"I'll do whatever I can. I talked to her grandmother, and I'm going to move in with them when I get home on break, then Brenda's going to help out after I come back here."

"Good." Debbie picked up one of Tiffany's bags. "Ready?"

"More than ready."

Betsy waited in the car. She had first met Tiffany when she was just a few weeks old, but they hadn't seen each other in at least two years. Betsy got out of the car and greeted Tiffany with, "It's good to see you again, but I'm so sorry about your friend." She got in the back seat, refusing to listen to any of Tiffany's reasons for sitting in front. "Debbie's sick of my jabbering, and I'm tired. I'd much rather sit here and eavesdrop on you two and maybe take a catnap."

As Debbie drove south, she asked questions about classes, finals, and friends. Anything to keep Tiffany's mind from dwelling on Ashling. It worked for half an hour.

"What was she doing out that early in the morning?" Tiffany's question popped up in the first lull they'd had in conversation since they'd left Cleveland.

Debbie glanced in the rearview mirror. She didn't want to get into the topic of Ashling's involvement in the theft with an audience in the back seat. But Betsy was sound asleep. "I think she might have been doing a job, working for someone." Should she say more? "When was the last time you talked to her?"

"The day before the accident. We were making plans to get together that Saturday when she and her grandma were supposed to be in Ravenna for her great-grandparents' anniversary."

"I just met her great-grandmother. She's a friend of Ray Zink, the man I bought my house from. What do you know about her?" It hadn't crossed Debbie's mind until now to question why Janet hadn't known the connection between her daughter's best friend's great-grandmother and the depot bench. But as the thought formed, she realized she couldn't name her own best friend's great-grandparents. She'd met Janet's maternal great-grandmother once when they were kids, but all she remembered was a tiny white-haired lady who used a walker.

"I know I met her a couple of times, but all I remember is that there's a picture of her at the museum. She was a Salvation Army volunteer in World War II. Oh, and their initials are carved on the bench. Any leads on who took it yet?"

The question made Debbie's neck tense. The doctors hadn't wanted Ashling to start talking for at least twenty-four hours. When had that time clock started? She had to do something to try to get to the bottom of this, and the best place to start was with Eileen. The text from Sonya had confirmed that she was involved.

Debbie answered Tiffany's question simply. "Not many." Then she kept the conversation light the rest of the way home.

When she parked in front of Ian and Janet's, Tiffany opened the door and flew up the walk. Debbie turned to see Betsy awake, watching the scene as Janet stepped out the door and opened her arms wide. She could only imagine what that image was doing to the heart of a mother who would never get to do that again. "Want to come in? Janet would love to see you, and I'm pretty sure there will be something sweet and delicious."

"You don't have to ask me twice. I'd love to see Janet and Ian."

After greetings and hugs, Janet told everyone to settle in the family room. She'd made one of Tiffany's favorites, monkey bread, and just needed to drizzle it with frosting before serving. Debbie offered to make coffee, grateful for a chance to talk to Janet alone.

As she popped a pod into the coffee maker and Janet swirled a stream of thin vanilla glaze over the mound of caramel pull-apart rolls, Debbie relayed everything she'd learned in the past two days, ending with, "I think it's time to confront our senior suspects. If they admit to hiring Ashling, she'll be cleared. If they've been keeping secrets from us, I'm pretty sure they'll come clean if they know what's at stake."

"Good plan. The sooner the better."

Janet picked up a stack of napkins then carried the picture-perfect monkey bread into the next room. Debbie set one cup of coffee aside, started another, and then pulled her phone out of her pocket. Before texting, she looked at the clock on the stove. It was just after three. If they got back to her house by four, she might have time to introduce Betsy to Rachel and Susannah, get her settled in her room, and start supper before their prime suspects at Good Shepherd left the dining room. She wanted to get there while they were all still sitting together.

Ian came in to the kitchen help her, and she asked him for permission to ask them her questions. After a reminder to instruct them not to tell anyone what they knew about Ashling's role, he gave her a green light. With more than a little amusement in his tone, he said, "Call me when you have enough evidence to arrest them."

Thinking Kim would want to be in on this, she called her after Ian left the room with cream and sugar.

"Hi, Deb. How was your trip?"

"Fun. And profitable. I'll tell you all about it tomorrow, but right now I'm wondering if you're free to meet me at Good Shepherd around five to talk to your mom and Ray. I need to know if they've learned anything more about what happened to the bench. There's been some new evidence, and they might be able to help solve this."

"Absolutely. Maybe they'll come clean about all this secrecy."

Debbie was amazed at the way the three women in her house clicked within minutes. By the time she walked out the door, Betsy was browning meat for tacos, Susannah was shredding lettuce, and Rachel was chopping tomatoes.

As she drove to Good Shepherd, she once again imagined the Bench Bandit suspects as actors in a movie. No matter what their reasons were, if they'd hired Ashling to remove the bench, their actions would make a great comedy. If they were complicit, the theft was far more funny than nefarious.

And that brought her back to reasons. What was their motive? Had Floyd, from the gas station, really convinced all of them that the bench disappearing, hopefully temporarily, would be good for business?

She parked and met Kim at the front door. Kim gave her a slightly lopsided grin. "This should be interesting. I can't wait to hear what they have to say for themselves."

Debbie laughed. "Pretty sure they've reached the age where they can get away with almost anything."

"I kind of hate to mess with whatever they're cooking up, don't you? If it's some kind of Christmas surprise…"

"I know." The thought had occurred to Debbie. Whatever they were up to, she was sure they had no intentions of anything bad resulting. "But it's kind of time sensitive that we find out what they know." When Kim shot her a questioning look, she told her about seeing Ashling in the surveillance video.

Kim's lips parted as she listened. "I absolutely cannot believe Ashling would do anything underhanded. I can, however, imagine my mom and her buddies doing something like this as a joke. But it's been over a week. Wouldn't they have accomplished their purposes by now?" She took a deep breath edged with frustration and squared her shoulders. "I'm just going to come right out and ask."

Kim led the way to the dining room where Eileen, Ray, and Madeline sat at a round table. To Debbie's surprise, Floyd and Harry, who both still lived on their own, were also there.

Kim walked up to the table, and Eileen looked up, startled, but clearly delighted to see her. "What a nice surprise. I didn't know you were coming back."

After bending to kiss her mother on the cheek, Kim said, "I have a question. For all of you." Her gaze swept the group. "Did you take, or hire someone to take, the depot bench?"

The expressions of confusion on the five faces were almost identical.

"What? You think *we* took it?" Harry asked. He was joined by the others pitching in to add, "Why would you think that?" and "What in the world would we want that old thing for?"

"I know you've been up to something," Kim said.

At that moment, Sonya walked over and stood beside her. "Me too. I've heard you talking about the bench, and you're always trying to meet in secret."

It was Debbie's turn to add her input. "Harry, I overheard you and Pete at the gas station talking about the bench, and then, Floyd, you came in and warned them that I…was…" Her words slowed as first Madeline and Eileen and then the men began snickering and then laughing in a way that only the word *guffawing* could describe.

"We…" Eileen wiped her eyes and pressed a hand to her chest. "We weren't plotting the theft of the bench."

Floyd shook his head and, hand shaking as he laughed, gestured to Madeline, who bent down and pulled something from a briefcase leaning against the leg of her chair. She handed a sheaf of papers to Kim. There were two photographs printed on the top one. The first, in black-and-white, showed a smiling twentysomething Eileen handing a doughnut to a young, uniformed Harry. The color picture next to it was a re-creation…eighty years later. The next page was a January calendar.

As Kim slowly paged through, Debbie felt her eyes sting. "You're making a calendar," she whispered, emotion tightening her voice. Then she realized she needed to say it again, much louder.

Madeline nodded. "We wanted to do something for the depot restoration fund. It's ready to go to the printer. We're just waiting to take our Christmas picture." She held out another photo, one Debbie had seen a few days earlier. Black-and-white, a bit fuzzy due to falling snow. Three women seated on the bench in front of the depot and three men on the sides…while another was shown looking away, in silhouette, as if caught in the photo by accident, yet sporting a wide, goofy grin on his face. Exactly like the one he wore now…eighty years later.

CHAPTER TWENTY-THREE

On Tuesday afternoon, Debbie sat at her kitchen table with Betsy, Rachel, and Susannah, sipping tea and munching on still-warm Cajun-spiced pecans. "Blue eyes, huh?" Rachel gave her a teasing smile. "How blue?"

Debbie looked back at the woman who'd lost her husband a matter of weeks ago and was now peppering her with questions about Greg, telling her life was short and she needed to "Go for it." She searched for words to express how much that touched her, but the silly expressions on the faces of the other two women told her this wasn't the time. Susannah's face seemed lit with the enjoyment of teasing her. "I think you should ask him out for dinner. We'll be fine here."

Betsy, her smile unhindered by past sadness, nodded her approval. "We can put off going to the cemetery until tomorrow."

But… Today was the day. The anniversary of Reed's death. She and Betsy needed closure. This was the beginning of something new. "Let's still go to the cemetery, and then, if we're both feeling okay about it…maybe…" Looking down to hide her smile, Debbie picked up a glazed pecan and held it up for inspection. "These are amazing."

"And addictive," Betsy added.

"One of Mom's specialties," Susannah said. "If you think these are good, you need to try her pralines. And her Creole bacon, and crab cakes, and cheesy biscuits, and—"

"Susannah." Smiling, Rachel stopped her daughter's gushing with a hand on her arm.

"No, go on. Please." Debbie snagged another handful. "I want to hear more. Actually, I want to eat more. Have you ever made appetizers for a crowd?"

Susannah gave a vigorous nod. "She made the entire meal for my senior banquet."

"I *planned* it," Rachel said, looking uncomfortable under all the attention directed at her. "I had a lot of help. Including my daughter's."

"Can we hire you for Saturday?" Debbie told them about their "Who Stole Christmas?" party.

"That sounds like so much fun. We'd love to."

A knock at the front door caused Debbie's mood to shift. "That would be Greg." Though she looked forward to spending time with him, she dreaded the reason for it. At Ian's suggestion, they were going to visit Ashling. Debbie had protested, not wanting to upset her while she was recovering. "It's important to us," she'd said, "but it's just a piece of furniture. Ashling's fragile. I don't want to upset her right now. She's not going anywhere. Can't this wait?"

His answer had made sense. "It's not about discovering who's responsible. Sooner or later, she's going to find out what we know. Try as we might to keep it quiet, these things always get out. For her sake, I'd rather she heard it from someone she trusts." Then he said, "Let's try a gentle approach. Tell her what you saw on the security video and let her know you assume she had a legitimate, legal reason for picking up the bench."

On top of her anxiety about talking to Ashling, and in spite of Betsy's reassurances, Debbie had qualms about introducing Greg to the mother of the man she had planned to marry.

Debbie opened the door and was surprised when Greg stepped in and gave her a hug. A hug that lasted a bit longer than a common expression of greeting. She led him into the kitchen and made the necessary introductions. Though she'd told him on the phone who he'd be meeting, it still felt awkward. To her surprise, Betsy took the hand he offered and laid her other hand on top of his. A blessing.

After a few minutes of chitchatting, they said their goodbyes and got into Greg's car. "What time do you need to be home? I'm wondering if we could maybe stop for coffee after the hospital."

"There's something I have to do when we get back." Could she be as bold as her houseguests had told her to be? "But…I'm free for supper." There, she'd said it.

Greg glanced across the seat then flipped on his turn signal and pulled to the curb.

What was he thinking? Was this where they'd have the "just friends" talk? Had she misread the signals? Was he not—

"I'm calling Jaxon to a take a lasagna out of the freezer because they're going to be on their own tonight." He winked at her then placed the call.

Well then. He pulled away from the curb and kept driving. When he stopped at the stop sign at the corner of Center and Third Street, she said, "What's your favorite—Greg, look." She pointed at a pale green vintage pickup truck heading south, away from the intersection.

She didn't need to say another word. Greg turned left and, keeping a good distance, followed the truck, making a left turn onto Logan Street and then heading south again on Sixth. After about a mile, the truck turned into a gravel drive and drove behind a detached garage. Greg slowed the car, and Debbie's pulse quickened. Finally, after a tense minute, he said, "I don't think we should follow."

"I agree. Let's get the address and give it to Ian." The fire number at the end of the driveway was hidden by the limb of a fallen tree. "Drive up to the mailbox. Maybe it's on the front." The sun had slipped behind the trees, making visibility difficult, but when they got within a couple of feet, she was able to make out the faded letters where there had once been decals. "B-L-A…" And then the rest became clear. "Blackwell."

It wasn't just the medicinal smell of the hospital that was making Debbie feel queasy and a bit dizzy. Everything seemed off-kilter, including her recall of every conversation she'd had about the missing bench in the past ten days. Somebody had to be lying.

The bench, ordered by Jesse Blackwell in 1943, had been stolen eighty years later by the man's great-granddaughter, who now lay in a hospital bed.

Had the Good Shepherd Gang used their calendar project as a cover-up? Was Margie in on it? Debbie had looked up "Blackwell" along with the address on her phone and found that a Quinn

Blackwell, age seventy-four, lived in the house the green truck had taken them to. Quinn was Margie and Jesse's son and Ashling's great-uncle. Not a very close relationship. And the hooded man in the video had to be much younger, closer to Ashling's age, by the way he'd moved. Who was he? What was their motive? They'd appeared to be laughing in the grainy video footage. What if they'd been yelling instead?

Ian met them at the elevator on Ashling's floor. "I talked to her for a few minutes. I just asked for anything she could remember about the accident. She thinks she hit a patch of black ice going around a corner and lost control."

Debbie closed her eyes for a moment, trying not to picture the accident or how much worse it could have been.

"I'll wait just inside the door," Ian said. "She won't know I'm there. Don't feel like you have to push it. Tell her what you know, and let her take it from there."

Ashling, whose freckled complexion and bright green eyes were usually glowing, was as pale as the sheets she lay on except for the greenish-purple bruise surrounding her left eye and another on her arm. Her left leg was in a cast, and a bandage covered one side of her scalp. She turned her head slowly toward them and managed a wan smile. "Hi, Mr. Connor, Miss Debbie. Thank you for bringing Tiff home for the weekend." Her voice was low and hoarse.

"Being with you probably helped her as much as it did you. She's been worried."

Ashling tried to nod, but it made her flinch.

Greg pulled two chairs close to the bed. "The whole church has been praying for you. Actually, the whole town."

"That's what my grandma said."

Debbie leaned forward. "Ashling, we need you to help clear up a mystery for us."

"O…kay."

"The bench in front of the depot went missing the same day as your accident."

"Yeah." A sad smile curved her lips. "I missed the surprise. I hope they got good pictures."

"Surprise?" Debbie and Greg spoke in tandem.

"For my great-grandparents' anniversary."

Debbie exchanged a look of bewilderment with Greg. "The bench was taken for their anniversary?"

"Yes." Ashling seemed to be studying their faces, trying to make sense of their confusion. "Michael said it was okay. Is there a problem?"

"Michael…Morgan?"

Ashling nodded. But Kim had talked to several members of the village board. They'd said no one had authorized its removal.

"Can you start from the beginning?" Greg asked. "Why did you take it, and who helped you?"

Ridges formed on the pale skin above Ashling's brows. She looked at Debbie. "My cousin Cal saw the postcard you sent out, and that gave him the idea. My great-grandparents used to have their picture taken on the bench every year on their anniversary. Since my great-grandpa can't travel very far anymore, Cal said we should take the bench to them. At first it was kind of a joke, but the more we thought about it, the more it sounded like a fun idea. Cal is a great photographer. We were going to surprise them with the bench and do a photo shoot at their old house in Ravenna on Friday then have the pictures on display for the party on Saturday. I suppose it sounds kind of wild, but moving furniture is kinda my thing, and Cal has helped me on a lot of jobs."

"But you didn't use your truck," Debbie said.

"I had a job Friday morning, so Cal took the bench in his truck, and I was supposed to meet him, but…" Her expression darkened.

Debbie wanted to spare her from dwelling on what happened next. "And you cleared it with Michael Morgan?"

Ashling nodded then closed her eyes, clearly tiring. "He texted from Aruba and said we could take it as long as we returned it the same day, before the first Dennison Christmas train." She opened her eyes and stared quizzically at Greg and then Debbie. "What's going on? Why is this such a big deal?"

Debbie leaned in. "Ashling, do you know where the bench is now?"

"Where? Isn't it… You mean Cal didn't bring it back?"

"No. It's gone."

Ashling opened her eyes wide then squeezed them shut. "Was Cal in the truck with me?" Her voice quivered.

"No, honey." Debbie reached out to hold her hand. "You were alone, in your own truck. We can talk about this another time if—"

"No. I need to know what happened to Cal. Is he okay?"

Greg took Ashling's other hand. "We haven't heard anything. Would your grandmother know how to reach him?"

Ashling gave a slight nod then winced. "Cal is on the autism spectrum. He can follow instructions well, but he can't always problem solve. Maybe, after he heard the news about me, he didn't know what to do next."

"But Michael Morgan knew about it?"

"Yes. We would never… So nobody said anything? Did you think it was just stolen? How did you know I helped take it?"

Debbie stroked Ashling's hand, trying to quell her agitation. She told her about the security camera across from the depot. "It's been kind of a fun mystery, but you've solved it now. I'll talk to your grandma, and we'll find Cal and get the bench brought back."

Ashling closed her eyes and seemed to sink deeper into her pillow. "I'm sorry." A tear rolled down her cheek, but then a tiny smile teased one corner of her mouth. "You know"—she opened her eyes and looked at Debbie—"this is all your fault."

"*Mine*?"

"Yep. Well, yours and Janet's." Her smile widened. "I got distracted. The last thing I remember thinking before my truck spun out is that before I headed up to Ravenna, I needed to stop at the café and get some cake doughnuts for my great-grandma because it would be like giving her a little taste of home."

Debbie stood in front of the bathroom mirror, applying a second coat of mascara. A touch of blush and a swipe of lipstick, and she was ready. More ready for this than she would have been four days ago.

Two hours ago, she'd stood arm in arm with Betsy in Grandview Union Cemetery. The sun, low and orange on the horizon, had cast golden rays between stone monuments as they'd looked down at the inscription in white marble that represented the sadness they'd shared for twenty years.

REED JONATHAN BRANDT

MEDAL OF HONOR

SSG

US ARMY

AFGHANISTAN

APRIL 9, 1978

DECEMBER 12, 2003

"We were blessed," Betsy had whispered.

"Yes, we were." Debbie bent and placed a single red rose in front of the stone. "We both had something many people never get to experience."

After a moment of silence, Betsy was the first to pull away. "Now, let's get on with the business of living. And the first thing on our agenda is getting you ready for your date."

They'd chatted nonstop on the drive from Strasburg to Dennison, the conversation ping-ponging from what Debbie should wear to Betsy's new beau then to Greg, his boys, the café and the Grinch party, and on to thoughts about what the future might hold for both of them.

Debbie zipped her makeup bag and took a final look in the full-length mirror. While she would have gravitated to her dressiest jeans, Susannah had convinced her to wear one of the few winter dresses she owned, a long-sleeve, high-neck green knit with a wide leather belt. Her three handmaidens had raided her jewelry box and chosen a necklace consisting of three flat gold chains, and a matching bracelet. Debbie fluffed her short, dark hair with her fingertips then smiled in the mirror and opened the door…to an audience. Betsy, Rachel, and Susannah applauded as she stepped out, twirled, then curtsied.

The doorbell rang, and Susannah squealed. With a laugh bordering on a giggle, Debbie shushed her, took a deep breath, and opened the door.

Greg grinned then looked over her shoulder at their cheering section. "Evening, ladies."

"Good evening," they echoed. Betsy said, "Ladies, I think something's burning in the kitchen." On cue, they all turned on their heels and left.

Debbie took her coat from the front closet, and Greg helped her into it. She smiled up at him. "A girl could get used to this."

He laughed. "Maybe she should."

Late on Christmas Eve, Margie stood next to Andrea in front of an arched window in the Blackwells' Victorian home set on a hill, staring down at the Ravenna munitions plant. Andrea's father and Barry Cunningham stood directly behind them, both sighing nervously every few minutes.

This was the first Christmas Eve she hadn't spent with her parents. She'd promised to be home by noon tomorrow, but that hadn't eased the hurt in her mother's voice when Margie had called home on Sunday, four days ago, and said she was spending the week at Andrea's but couldn't tell them why. With Dutch overseas, Christmas was going to be hard enough on her parents, and now she'd compounded their sadness. But she needed to be here.

She thought back over the week. Listening outside the Blackwells' library door as Barry and Mr. Blackwell talked, then telling them everything they'd found in Jonathan's apartment. Mr. Blackwell's countenance had gone from shock to anger to something resembling pride. "You could have been killed," he'd said, drilling his daughter with his dark eyes. "But you may have saved hundreds of lives."

They'd only been allowed to hear bits and pieces of what was happening behind the scenes. Major Sterling had believed Barry's report. An hour ago, Mr. Blackwell had received a call. Army engineers had found more than five hundred pounds of TNT attached to the pilings under the Steubenville Bridge. There were tears in Mr. Blackwell's eyes when he told them.

Half a mile away, all was still. A full moon, reflecting on new-fallen snow, made their view clear. It was a peaceful scene. Deceptively calm. No movement to indicate that more than a dozen soldiers were in place. The plant had been thoroughly searched. No blasting caps or detonating devices had been found, which meant that someone was coming to detonate the explosives. If Jonathan and his accomplices were going to go ahead with their plan, it would likely unfold any minute now.

A glance at Andrea told her Margie was praying. Eyes closed, lips moving almost imperceptibly. The hall clock chimed eleven times. Another sigh from Mr. Blackwell, echoed by Barry. Andrea opened her eyes and grabbed Margie's hand.

Headlights turned onto the road leading to the plant. Margie squeezed Andrea's hand. "Lord, please..." she whispered. Barry put his hand on her shoulder.

Machine gun fire. A burst of light. The noise split the silence, followed by a ball of fire and shockwaves that rattled the windows. Margie held her breath, waiting for the fire to ignite a chain reaction in the buildings filled with ammunition. But the flames shrank.

"They did it," Mr. Blackwell whispered, his voice ragged. One arm slid around his daughter. The other pulled Margie and Barry into his large embrace. "You did it. You may never get public recognition for this, but what you did..." His voice cracked. "You are all heroes."

Margie stared at the flames and tried to feel like a hero, but all she could feel was numb.

Someone, possibly Jonathan Goldman, had been driving the truck that now burned low, lighting the night with an orange glow.

CHAPTER TWENTY-FOUR

$\mathcal{A}$n hour after turning over the Closed sign on Saturday afternoon, Debbie stood next to Janet in front of the depot as the ground beneath their feet began to vibrate with a familiar rumble. They stood in silence, watching the Dennison Christmas train leave the station. How many women over the years had stood on this platform, saying goodbye or waiting for someone they loved to return? Today, they weren't waiting for a train but a truck, and instead of a person, it was an object that held memories for both them and the entire community.

A ding from her phone brought her thoughts back to the present. She pulled it from her apron pocket. A text from Nathan. "Look." She held out the phone, and they read the words together.

No lives were lost at the Ravenna munitions plant on Christmas Eve, 1942. Because of actions by several heroic citizens, the culprits who intended to detonate explosives stored at the plant were apprehended, their truck and equipment destroyed, and no lives were lost or injuries reported. There is no way to calculate the number of lives saved.

The sound of tires on gravel made them both turn. A pickup truck with Connor Construction on the door drove up then backed toward them.

And there it was. Unbeknownst to anyone but Cal Blackwell, who had followed instructions but didn't know what to do next without Ashling's guidance, the bench had spent two weeks in a shed behind the house Jesse and Margie bought in Ravenna in 1949. The house was now occupied by one of their grandchildren and her family, but the shed was never used in the winter.

Both Kim and Ian had spoken to Michael Morgan, who claimed "vacation brain" as the reason he hadn't told any of the village board members about giving Ashling and Cal permission to take the bench. No charges were filed. Before bringing it back home, Greg and his boys, with help from several nursing home aides, had taken Jesse and Margie to the house, where Jaxon had done a photo shoot to commemorate their eightieth anniversary.

"Home sweet home," Greg said as he, Jaxon, and Julian maneuvered the bench into place and fastened it down with new bolts. Debbie wiped it down, pausing over names and dates as she did. Janet was ready with the greenery and bright red bows to attach to the ends, just the way Madeline's mother-in-law had done decades ago.

Before Jaxon had time to finish setting up his lights and tripod, they had their first customers. Two families approached, both with children in pajamas, and Jaxon gave them instructions, posing them much like the family in the promotional postcard that had started the whole bench mystery.

Greg put an arm across Debbie's shoulders. "You go get all your Grinchy food ready. Julian and I will direct traffic and get the names and email addresses of everyone who has their picture taken."

She leaned into him. "Thank you." Then she and Janet went inside to finish hanging decorations. With the help of Ian and several of his men, they'd set up the buffet line in the café and arranged round tables in the depot waiting area that were now covered with red tablecloths. At each table were the booklets of stories Debbie had collected, and each place was decorated with a Grinch-green bow with white polka dots and a candy cane tied in the center. In the middle of each table sat an arrangement of lime-green and red ribbon curlicues and satin balls surrounding pillar candles in glass holders, all done by Tiffany and Susannah at Ashling's house that morning. They'd created beauty while forging a friendship that had all the makings of a lifelong bond.

By six o'clock, a crowd of people in ugly Christmas sweaters and Grinch costumes milled around, sampling and exclaiming over Rachel's appetizers. Debbie looked at Janet. "Is it time?"

"Yep. I'll go get Pastor Nick to pray, and then—"

"Janet! Debbie!" Greg came rushing in, out of breath. "You'll want to see this." He motioned toward the door, and they followed.

Once outside, Debbie gasped, and Janet echoed her. Three women sat on the bench. Harriet Woodson, Eileen Palmer, and Margie McGarry Blackwell. Floyd Marsh and Pete Kimball flanked one side. Ray Zink sat on the other, in his wheelchair. Harry stood to one side, facing away, grinning like the Cheshire cat. "All we need now is snow!" Debbie exclaimed.

Jaxon snapped dozens of pictures, then Eileen motioned to Madeline, who stood taking her own pictures, tears glistening in her eyes. "Now let's get one with you," Eileen said. "You can't always hide behind a camera, you know."

As they posed again, another photographer stepped up behind Jaxon. This one wore a jacket with Ohio Heritage Magazine printed on the front.

As Debbie moved toward the microphone, Harry waved at her, beckoning her to his table. She walked over and crouched down beside him.

Harry held out a piece of paper. "As hard as it is to admit, my ex-grandson-in-law isn't all bad. Kim just gave me this."

Debbie took the page. A printed email. *Got back yesterday and heard about the bench. So very sorry I didn't follow through, and I apologize for my nephew. I know how much the bench means to this town. Glad to hear it's all been resolved. On behalf of my family, I'll be sending a sizable donation to the depot restoration fund.*

With a hand on Harry's shoulder, Debbie gave the paper back to him. "Goes to show we are all capable of change, doesn't it?"

"I will begrudgingly admit you might be right." Harry's face crinkled as he winked at her.

Debbie walked to the microphone. "Could I have your attention, please?" She cleared her throat, still a bit raw from the emotion elicited by the re-created photo shoot. "I have a couple of announcements before we eat. First, as you know, a reward was offered for information leading to the recovery of the missing bench. We are now pleased to give that money to someone most of you know." She gestured to Janet, who held up an envelope and walked to the corner of the room where Tiffany and Susannah stood behind Margie, who was sitting in her wheelchair. "Ashling Kelly, thank you for your help, and we hope this tides you over until you're back on your feet and we can all once again hire Jill of All Trades to move us, clean up our messes, and fix our mistakes."

The crowd erupted in applause as Ashling's mouth dropped open and she shook her head and began to cry. As "No" formed on her lips, Janet bent down and whispered in her ear and Margie reached for her great-granddaughter's hand and said something Debbie couldn't hear but she knew was a blessing. After a minute, Ashling nodded, looked at Debbie, and mouthed, "Thank you."

"Secondly," Debbie said, "I'd like everyone to welcome the photographers from *Ohio Heritage* magazine, who are here to capture our unique Dennison Christmas spirit." She held her hands out from her sides, palms up. "But I think we can all agree that no matter what the results of the contest are, we wouldn't trade Dennison and our Christmas memories here for all the prizes in the world!"

After the applause and shouts of affirmation died down, she said, "Now I'd like to ask Pastor Nick Winston to pray for our meal."

Pastor Nick stepped in front of the banquet table. "Father God, we come before You tonight with deep gratitude. In this building rich with history, in a town known as 'A great place to call home,' we thank You for Your provision and protection over the years. Though tonight we're enjoying some lighthearted fun, we are not forgetting the reason we celebrate this season, the gift of Your Son, Jesus. Thank You now for this food and the hands that have prepared it. We ask Your blessing upon our words and our time together. Amen."

As the room filled with Christmas music from the 1940s, Debbie took her place next to Janet, ready to refill pans of Roast Beast, Who Hash, Mount Crumpit Noodles, Grinch Greens, and Cindy Lu Salad. The last person in the buffet line was Rita Carson. "May I have a word?" she asked.

Debbie shot a quick glance at Janet and simultaneously prayed for peace. "Of course." Rita motioned for them to follow her then led the way to the table where Doris Kimball sat with her father. "I have something to say." Rita twisted a red paper napkin in her hands. "I would like to bury the hatchet, Doris. I caused a fuss about that old bench years ago, and it drove a wedge between us. I admit my reasons were selfish. I won't go into that now, but the past two weeks have shown me I was wrong. This town needs reminders of where we've been and what we can learn from our past. I'm so very sorry for everything."

Doris rose from her chair and wrapped her ample arms around a stiff and surprised Rita. "I'm ashamed of the way I acted back then too. Let's agree to move on."

Rita, overcome with emotion she didn't seem to know what to do with, simply nodded. Debbie rested a hand on her shoulder. Her heart went out to this woman whose past was filled with far more bitter than sweet. "All is forgiven, Rita. Now let's fill up our plates and enjoy the evening. Would you like to sit with us?"

"Me?"

Rita's incredulous expression would have been comical if it wasn't so sad. Was she really so used to being rejected that this simple invitation shocked her? "Of course, you. I have some people I'd like you to meet." Debbie handed Rita a plate and pointed to a table where Ian, Greg, Jaxon, Julian, Rachel, and Susannah sat. "Right over there."

By the time they got to their table with full plates, there were tears in Rita's eyes. "Thank you," she said, voice rough with emotion, then held out her hand to Rachel. "Hi." A smile, maybe her first in a very long time, lit her face. "I'm Rita Carson."

Rachel answered with a matching smile, and Debbie leaned close to Janet and whispered, "I think we're witnessing a real-life Grinch story."

After the ugly sweater and costume contest winners were announced, and Janet had cut and served her three-tier red-and-green cake, Debbie sat back and simply listened to the laughter and chatter.

When Kate Smith's rich voice over the speakers began to sing "Silent Night," the room quieted, and someone began to sing along. Soon the whole room joined in. When they reached the last stanza, Debbie's eyes stung with tears of gratitude. *Silent night, holy night! Son of God, love's pure light…* The song ended, and Jaxon interrupted the silence with a single word—"Snow!"—that brought a cheer from the crowd. Outside the large windows, snowflakes danced in the depot lights, covering the ground…and the bench.

Greg put his arm across her shoulders as Jaxon held up his phone and the notes of a perfectly fitting old song drifted out of it. Debbie smiled up at Greg and then joined everyone as they sang. *Yes*, Debbie thought, basking in the warmth of the roomful of old and new friends. *Let it snow.*

December 23, 1953

"Jammie time!" Margie called over the din of three children playing Pick-Up Sticks on their bedroom floor. "Colleen, Annie, Quinn, we can go as soon as everyone gets their pajamas on. Hot chocolate and cookies at Aunt Eileen's house right after pictures at the depot."

Like every year, getting her brood dressed for the ride to Dennison, then keeping them clean and happy until after their annual Christmas picture was taken, was a major undertaking. One she would never tire of. As she handed out three pairs of matching footy pajamas, strong arms wrapped around her from behind. She smiled and leaned into Jesse. "Merry Christmas," he whispered in her ear.

She turned, still encircled in his embrace, and kissed him. "Merry Christmas." Something rustled in his hand. She looked down to see an envelope. "What's that?"

Without a word, he held out the unopened letter. From Jonathan Goldman.

With trembling hands, Margie opened it, and they read in silence.

Dear Jesse and Margie,

This letter is long overdue, but I am finally writing to say thank you. Jesse, I will be forever grateful for the tenacity you and Barry showed by going around your father to get to the truth. Margie, thank you for the courage and conviction that enabled you and Andrea to steal my key and search my apartment. If it were not for you, I, and those I worked for, would likely have been successful. Though the cause seemed just at the time, I weep now to think of the damage, setbacks, and likely loss of life that would have resulted.

If it were not for you, I would never have been alone in a cell with nothing but the Bible and a letter of undeserved grace and forgiveness you sent me. Though it took years for your kindness and God's truth to pierce my pride, I finally met Jesus. Because of seeing "Love your enemies and pray for those who persecute you" in action in you, I have been able to forgive those who brainwashed me into thinking that an act of pure evil was good and right.

Because of you, I would rather be here, calling a prison cell home at Christmas, than back in the country of my birth with blood on my hands and guilt on my shoulders. Because of you, I can rejoice in this season and look for opportunities to share Christ with those around me. May God bless you and your precious family this Christmas and always.

With deepest gratitude,

Jonathan

Dear Reader,

Have you ever been through a season where you needed to "press on"?

I love reading (and writing) stories of the Greatest Generation... men and women whose lives were turned upside down by something beyond their control, who responded by rolling up their sleeves. Young men enlisted. Women and older men planted victory gardens or held scrap drives. Women sewed parachutes, built bombers, joined the Women's Army Corps or the Women's Land Army, or, like Margie, Madeline, and Eileen, gave soldiers far from family a little taste of home. During World War II, 1.3 million service members were served free food by 4,000 working volunteers at the Dennison Depot Salvation Army Servicemen's Canteen.

After the war these men and women, who had lost loved ones and sacrificed in innumerable other ways, picked up the pieces and began rebuilding their lives. Debbie was right. Kids today still need to hear about heroes. Real, true heroes. Flawed people who step up and do the right thing at the right time in spite of obstacles.

I pray our country never again has to face the kind of global conflict these men and women endured, but even in our everyday lives we have opportunities to "press on," with God's help, through prejudice, injustice, and even our own personal battles with grief, bitterness, selfishness, and pride. We can leave a legacy for future generations in the small daily decisions we make as we join the apostle Paul in saying, "...But one thing I do: Forgetting what is behind and straining toward what is ahead, I press on toward the goal to win the prize for which God has called me heavenward in Christ Jesus" (Philippians 3:13–14). I hope the World War II stories—both real and fiction-based-in-reality—included in the Whistle Stop Café Mysteries inspire you to do just that.

God bless,
Becky Melby

ABOUT the AUTHOR

Becky Melby writes contemporary women's fiction, time-slip novels, and cozy mysteries. Becky and her husband, Bill, call Wisconsin home. They are the parents of four sons and have fifteen grandchildren. When not writing or spoiling grandchildren, Becky may be found riding on the back of their Honda Gold Wing motorcycle or touring the country in their RV.

A GLIMPSE of the PAST

German Saboteurs in America

Did you know that during World War II, there were German saboteurs on American soil? Ultimately, they were unsuccessful, and important infrastructure and countless lives were saved. Here's that story.

Intent on destroying the United States economy as well as the morale of the American people, who were sending huge numbers of troops at enormous cost to fight in Europe, German military intelligence devised a plan. They located German men who had previously lived in the United States and understood American customs, and who might be able to blend in with the population while they carried out their missions.

They very nearly succeeded! In 1942, two German U-boats surfaced in the Atlantic: one near Long Island and one in Florida. Four trained German saboteurs were rowed to the mainland and stepped onto American soil at each location, all eight outfitted with cash, maps, and detailed—and completely fictional—new American-citizen identities, right down to fake letters from American "relatives." The men were tasked with blowing up roads, bridges, railways, electrical plants, and factories in an effort to keep the Americans from changing the tide of the war.

But thanks to the keen eyes of a Coast Guard agent, one group was apprehended before damage could be done. The other group was thwarted when one of the saboteurs turned himself in to the FBI and revealed the plot.

The following year, as so often happens, Hollywood got involved in history. The movie *They Came to Blow Up America*, starring George Sanders as an undercover American spy, was a mostly fictionalized telling of this failed German operation.

FROM the HOME-FRONT KITCHEN

Debbie's Creamed Chicken

Ingredients:

⅓ cup butter

⅓ cup all-purpose flour

2 cups rich chicken broth

2 cups half-and-half or heavy
    cream

½ teaspoon garlic powder

½ teaspoon dried thyme

Salt to taste

Pepper to taste

3 cups cooked chicken

¾ cup toasted slivered
    almonds

Directions:

Melt butter in large saucepan over medium heat. Add flour, stirring well. Slowly pour in broth and half-and-half, stirring constantly, then add garlic powder, thyme, salt, and pepper. Bring to a boil, decrease heat, and simmer until thickened. Add chicken and almonds. Serve over biscuits or egg noodles.

*Read on for a sneak peek of another exciting book
in the Whistle Stop Café Mysteries series!*

ACCENTUATE
THE POSITIVE

BY JEANETTE HANSCOME

Janet Shaw unzipped her coat in the homey warmth of Aunt
Maggie's Antiques and Consignment. Getting there had required
her husband, Ian, to drive only a few miles outside Dennison, but on
this first Sunday after putting away everything holiday related, it felt
like an exciting post-Christmas road trip.

She took a business card from the welcome table near the door
of what had once been a Victorian house. "Debbie will love this
place," she said to Ian. "Too bad we didn't know about it during the
holidays. I bet it was adorable."

Janet had stumbled upon Aunt Maggie's online while helping
her daughter Tiffany search for an affordable pair of boots for a spur-
of-the-moment ski trip. It looked even better than in the pictures. A
fire burned in a woodstove in the corner. A few feet away, a round
table covered with a royal-blue tablecloth welcomed customers with
a plate of cookies and thermoses marked *hot apple cider* and *coffee*.

Janet took her husband's hand. "Thanks for getting me out today."

Ian gave her hand a gentle squeeze. "The house felt too quiet to me too."

Janet examined the contents of a square glass case near the cookie table. It held more expensive antique jewelry and watches. "I guess it's the price we pay for having a daughter who knows how to make friends."

Tiffany would still be at home on winter break if not for a call from her college roommate, who'd invited her to take a sick friend's place on the ski trip. "At least she's having fun before second-semester classes start."

A slender middle-aged woman sitting behind the cash register put aside her kitting. "Is there anything special you're looking for?"

Janet picked up a rose-printed teacup to admire the pattern. "Just browsing. Are you Aunt Maggie?"

"No. Maggie was my aunt. My great-aunt, technically. My husband and I bought this house from her family after she passed away. I'm Anne."

Ian helped himself to a cup of hot cider. "You have a nice place here."

"Thank you."

Enticed by the sweet aroma of Ian's cider, Janet poured herself some as well. "How long have you been open?"

"Just since June." Anne walked around to the front of the white cashier counter adorned with baskets of impulse buys. "You're one of the women who runs the Whistle Stop Café at the Dennison train station, aren't you?"

"Sure am. I'm Janet."

"My husband and I were there a few days before Christmas. I had some of your yummy gingerbread."

Janet made a mental note to make more gingerbread for the upcoming week. She wrapped her hands around the steaming cup of cider and breathed in the cinnamon-clove-infused goodness. "I hope you come back again."

"I'm sure I will." Anne returned to her chair and picked up her knitting. "Feel free to look around as long as you like."

Janet sipped her cider and ventured over to one of the side rooms while Ian thumbed through a trunk of old *Life* magazines.

The small room was set up like a den, with old books for sale on built-in shelves, tables of stationery and handmade journals, a cozy chair draped with throws, and a rolltop desk.

A portable lap desk with swirly carving along the edges sat smack dab in the middle of the open rolltop. It called to Janet. The lap desk even had two narrow drawers in front and a hole for an ink bottle.

Ian came in as she was searching for a price tag.

Janet reached for one of the drawers then noticed the *Please don't touch. Ask for assistance* card on top. "My grandmother had a porta-ble desk similar to this one. She used it for writing letters and cards for birthdays and holidays." She could still hear the *scritch scritch* of Grammy's Parker fountain pen, her favorite tool for letter writing.

Ian finished off his cider and tossed his cup in a wastebasket beside the rolltop desk. "Did you see how much it costs?"

Janet shook her head and turned around to call for Anne. But Anne was already on her way over.

"I just set that out yesterday," she said. "I found it while I was putting away holiday decorations. I'm sure it belonged to someone in Aunt Maggie's family. I thought about keeping it, but if I held on to every lovely item I found among her things, our house would look like—" She waved one hand at the desk and the other toward a table stacked with vintage-style calendars. "Well, like this store. Cute, but no place to sit."

Janet put her hands behind her back to keep herself from breaking the *Please don't touch* rule. "Did you find anything interesting inside it?"

Anne's big brown eyes grew wide and bright. "It was a gold mine of old stationery and postcards." She lifted the lid that doubled as a writing surface, uncovering neat stacks of cards, paper, and envelopes. "I also found some photos and an old composition book with a lot of writing in it. Those I kept. But everything that was unused, I decided to include with the desk." Anne stepped aside. "You can touch it. I added the sign so kids wouldn't mistake it for an art station and make a mess."

Janet relaxed and opened one of the drawers. It contained a pack of multicolored gel pens and a small box of ballpoints. "I can see why kids might mistake this for an art station."

"I didn't want to offer all that stationery without something to write with." Anne picked up a small rectangular box beside the lap desk. "Look at this fun little treasure." She opened the box and took out a copper-colored pen. When she held it up to the light, a unique marble effect contrasted the copper. She unscrewed the cap. "It's a fountain pen."

Ian touched the barrel. "That's a unique color."

"Isn't it great? It works really well. I filled it with fresh ink and tried it out."

Janet took the pen from Anne to get a closer look. The *Parker* stamp on the clip immediately triggered a memory of her grandmother. Grammy's pen had been red. "You found this in the lap desk?" The gold nib was stamped with *Parker Duofold*, as was the side of the pen, so it wasn't exactly like Grammy's. But similar enough.

"I almost included it with the other pens, but I knew my husband would insist I sell it separately, so I found a box for it."

Janet set the pen back in the box and found a price on the side. Fifteen dollars.

Anne positioned the box in a way that caused the overhead light to shine on a partially rubbed off *M* in the *Made in USA* stamp. "I had to guess on the price until my husband returns from visiting his mom. He's the pen person. My specialty is china and old furniture."

Ian opened another drawer in the desk that contained more notecards. "Whoever owned this desk and pen really liked to write."

Janet went back to admiring the desk. She imagined it in the café, along with the copper fountain pen. "I wonder what Debbie would think of displaying these in the café. I know they aren't train-related, but—"

"You should go ahead and get them." Ian picked up the fountain pen. He took an old receipt out of his pocket and printed his name. "If Debbie doesn't think they're a good match for the café, we'll find a place for the desk at home, and you can use the fountain pen to write recipes the old-fashioned way." He handed it to Janet.

Janet poised it in the writing position. "That would be fun."

"You know what?" Anne shut the desk and pulled a price sticker off the back of it. "If you want both for the café, I'll knock off ten percent and throw in the bottle of refill ink I bought for the fountain pen."

Janet looked up at Ian and nodded.

"It's a deal," he said.

Anne smiled and picked up the little writing desk and the box containing the pen. "It won't hurt my feelings if you decide to toss the old stationery and use the other pens at the café. I just wanted the desk to look complete."

At the register, Janet ran her hands over the smooth wood of the desk and the intricate etchings along the sides, again hearing the scritch of her grandma writing letters to friends while her grandchildren played or watched television. She still had a few of the cards she'd received from Grammy—special ones that included notes that she treasured. She opened the lid, tucked the boxed fountain pen between the stacks of cards and envelopes, and said, "I think I know exactly what I want to do with the stationery."

The next morning, Janet slipped a red-and-white polka-dot apron over the I'M KIND OF A BIG DEAL sweatshirt that Tiffany had given her for Christmas. She went over to the lap desk that she'd placed on a rustic square table near the entrance of the café. The smell of fresh cinnamon rolls and gingerbread added an extra sense of comfort on a cold Monday morning.

Debbie Albright walked into the dining area from the kitchen. "I'm so glad Ian talked you into getting that. Thanks for sharing it with the café."

Janet reached behind the table and pulled out the part of the display she hadn't shared with Debbie yet. "I'm glad you like it. Because I have an idea." She held up a corkboard that had once hung in Tiffany's room covered with pictures of friends, favorite actors, school certificates, and postcards from family trips. "I think it'll be fun for customers, and even for us." She stood back to give Debbie room to fully take in her creation.

MAKE SOMEONE'S DAY IN THE DREARY MONTH OF JANUARY!
WRITE AN ENCOURAGING WORD, QUOTE, OR VERSE.
TACK IT TO THE BOARD FOR OTHERS TO ENJOY.
BE CREATIVE. ALL WE ASK IS THAT YOU KEEP IT
CLEAN AND UPLIFTING.

"This is great." Debbie took the board from her. She set it behind the desk and leaned it against the wall. "There. Now customers can start using it. We can hang it on the wall later to make it more secure."

Janet pushed a chair up to the table. "I cut the sheets of stationary in halves and fourths." She opened the drawer that Anne had filled with pens. "If customers don't go for it, we can post encouraging notes of our own." She opened both packs of pens, selected a few from each, and dropped them into the hole that would have held an ink bottle back in the day. She retrieved a container of tacks from another drawer and set it beside the desk. Then she opened the desk to reveal the pièce de résistance—the wooden box containing her gorgeous fountain pen. She lifted the lid with a flourish. "Ta-da! I wrote a card to my parents with it last night to try it out. It was so fun."

"Are you sure you want to put that out? It looks pretty fancy."

"Sure I'm sure. What's the fun of having a pretty pen if it never gets used?"

"True enough." Debbie flipped the Closed sign to Open. "I'll bring a quote book from home tomorrow in case people need some inspiration and want to copy one."

Janet found her phone and took a picture of the new writing station and the pen. She reached into her tote bag for the little sign she'd made.

PLEASE BE CAREFUL WHEN USING THE FOUNTAIN PEN.

Debbie slipped an order pad into the pocket of her apron. "This will be a perfect winter activity."

Janet peeked through the window to check for their first customer but didn't see anyone yet. She removed the cap from the fountain pen and took out a notecard. "I'll get us started."

She took a seat in the chair to write. The satisfying scratch of the pen's nib against the wood of the lap desk made her a little giddy inside, even though her penmanship wasn't nearly as lovely as Grammy's used to be. She took a tack out of the cup and stuck her note to the corkboard.

Give yourself a great day!

Patricia Franklin was the first regular to show up at the café. She rubbed her gloved hands together. "Whew, it is nippy out there."

Janet took her place behind the bakery case. "What are you in the mood for today besides your usual peppermint mocha? I have some cinnamon rolls straight from the oven, along with apple-spice muffins and the gingerbread that has been such a hit lately…"

Patricia rested her chin on her fingers and peered into the case. "Hmm. I've been hearing good things about your gingerbread."

"Gingerbread it is. Would you like some whipped cream on it?"

"Why not?"

Janet chatted with Patricia while plating her bread and preparing her mocha. "Do you have a busy day ahead of you?"

Patricia settled herself on a stool at the counter. The dramatic thud of her overstuffed tote bag hitting the stool beside her said it all. "The law profession doesn't stop for winter, that's for sure."

Janet sprayed an extra-large swirl of whipped cream on top of Patricia's bread and dusted her mocha with cocoa powder. "There you go. A little extra sweetness to get you going this morning."

Patricia licked her lips. "Mm. I should appear stressed more often." She looked around the empty dining area. Janet knew she'd noticed the writing station when Patricia said, "Aw. That note on your new board just made my morning."

Janet handed her a napkin. "Exactly what I was hoping for."

As Patricia savored her first bite of gingerbread, Janet spotted Harry Franklin and his friendly dog, Crosby, right outside the café, in the part of the depot that used to serve as an indoor waiting area.

As soon as Harry opened the door to come in, Crosby gave himself a shake, sending snow flying off his red tartan dog sweater and grayish-white coat. Harry pointed over his shoulder to the writing desk. "I like your new accessory." He went over for a closer look and picked up the fountain pen. "I used to have one of these." He waved to his granddaughter and returned the pen to its box. "Morning, Patricia."

Patricia wiped her lips with a napkin. "Morning, Pop Pop."

A white-haired woman Janet had never seen before came in behind Harry. It was hard to guess her age. With her posture, stylish purse, and colorful scarf, Janet guessed that she was one of those women who'd learned how to appear younger than she really was. She stopped to examine the writing desk and picked up the fountain pen before asking to be seated near the window. Harry gave her a friendly nod as Debbie escorted her to a table.

Janet took a mug off the tray behind her. "What can I get for you, Harry?"

He eyed Patricia's drink. "I'll take one of those peppermint mochas. You only live once."

Patricia raised her cup. "Amen." She reached down to pet Crosby. "Hey, boy. Don't you look handsome?"

Harry took a seat beside Patricia at the counter. "Can I get it in a to-go cup? I have a class this morning."

Janet started Harry's mocha. "That's so cool. Did you sign up for one of those art classes at the community center?" One of the things Janet loved most about Harry was his ability to enjoy a full life despite being in his midnineties.

"No, a nice lady named Kate Lipton is offering a free writing workshop every Monday and Wednesday morning for the next four weeks to help us old-timers tell our life stories. It meets at Good Shepherd, but all seniors in the community are welcome. Since I qualify, I thought I'd try it out."

Janet forced herself not to react to Harry's words. She hadn't heard the name Kate Lipton since Debbie lived in Cleveland and shared frequent stories about a woman by that name who attended the same church she did. Debbie's Kate Lipton ran a window and glass business with her husband and managed to be in charge of everything from Bible studies to the women's ministries newsletter. Could Harry be talking about a different Kate Lipton? Based on what she remembered about Debbie's old church acquaintance, Dennison wasn't her scene at all.

Debbie handed Janet the older woman's order for an apple-spice muffin and hot tea. As she did, she shot Janet a confused look. Janet guessed Debbie was thinking the same thing about the person Harry had called Kate Lipton.

Patricia stabbed her fork into her slice of gingerbread. "I'm proud of you, Pop Pop."

"So am I," the woman seated by the window said. "Never stop learning. That's my motto."

"See." Janet took a to-go cup off the stack beside the espresso maker. "Even first-time customers are impressed."

Debbie set a mug and a basket of tea bags in front of the woman by the window. "Let me know if you'd like more hot water."

Harry rubbed the top of Crosby's head and turned to face the newcomer. "I'm sure you can still sign up if you're interested. I didn't see anything about the workshop being full."

The corners of the woman's lips curved upward. She raised her eyebrow and picked up her mug. "Maybe I'll pop in sometime."

Janet handed the woman's muffin to Debbie then delivered Harry's to-go mocha. "You're an inspiration to us all, Harry Franklin."

"I don't know about that." Harry turned his face away, but not before Janet noticed his grin. "But I do think it'll be interesting to hear everyone's stories. Eileen and Ray signed up too. Who knows, we might learn some new things about each other."

The woman by the window broke her muffin in half. She alternated her attention between the writing desk and Harry.

Harry checked his watch. "Well, I better say goodbye. Class starts at ten sharp, and I still need to stop by the drugstore to buy a notebook. I don't want to be tardy." He reached into his pocket and pulled out his wallet.

Patricia held up her hand. "Put your money away. This one's on me. You used to buy me first-day-of-school treats. Now it's my turn."

Harry gave Patricia a peck on the cheek. "Why, thank you." He pointed his paper cup at the writing desk. "I look forward to adding something to the message board when I can think of a profound statement. Now that I'm a writer and all." He gripped Crosby's leash in his hand and led him to the door. "Come on, boy. Let's go tell some stories."

Janet ran a damp cloth over the milk frother so it would be clean for the next mocha or latte order. "Have fun, Harry. Oh, and if that fountain pen reminds you of one you once had, I'll let you borrow it to write one of your stories with it for old time's sake."

Harry took another look at the pen. "I think I will."

The woman by the window waved to Harry, and he waved back. A trickle of customers eager for morning coffee prevented Janet from going over to introduce herself. Paulette arrived just in time to help with the rush. By the time Janet had said goodbye to Patricia, served pastries and fancy coffees, and replenished the popular gingerbread, the woman had left. Enough cash to cover her tea, muffin, and a generous tip lay on the table under the sugar bowl. Janet handed the bills to Debbie. "I hope she comes back. She seemed like a nice woman."

Debbie took the money to the cash register. "And very interested in Harry."

Janet smiled. "It did look like she was watching him." She walked over to the writing station to see if anyone had left a note. Patricia had added one in blue gel pen.

The Whistle Stop Café is heaven on earth with extra sweetness.

She spotted another note in the middle of the board. "Debbie, you have to see this." She pointed to the cream-colored card with the perfect fountain-pen penmanship. "Look. It's for Harry."

While you are waiting for the next fascinating story in the Whistle Stop Café Mysteries, check out another Guideposts mystery series!

SAVANNAH SECRETS

Welcome to Savannah, Georgia, a picture-perfect Southern city known for its manicured parks, moss-covered oaks, and antebellum architecture. Walk down one of the cobblestone streets, and you'll come upon Magnolia Investigations. It is here where two friends have joined forces to unravel some of Savannah's deepest secrets. Tag along as clues are exposed, red herrings discarded, and thrilling surprises revealed. Find inspiration in the special bond between Meredith Bellefontaine and Julia Foley. Cheer the friends on as they listen to their hearts and rely on their faith to solve each new case that comes their way.

The Hidden Gate
A Fallen Petal
Double Trouble
Whispering Bells
Where Time Stood Still
The Weight of Years
Willful Transgressions

Season's Meetings
Southern Fried Secrets
The Greatest of These
Patterns of Deception
The Waving Girl
Beneath a Dragon Moon
Garden Variety Crimes
Meant for Good
A Bone to Pick
Honeybees & Legacies
True Grits
Sapphire Secret
Jingle Bell Heist
Buried Secrets
A Puzzle of Pearls
Facing the Facts
Resurrecting Trouble
Forever and a Day

A NOTE FROM the EDITORS

We hope you enjoyed another exciting volume in the Whistle Stop Café Mysteries series, published by Guideposts. For over seventy-five years, Guideposts, a nonprofit organization, has been driven by a vision of a world filled with hope. We aspire to be the voice of a trusted friend, a friend who makes you feel more hopeful and connected.

By making a purchase from Guideposts, you join our community in touching millions of lives, inspiring them to believe that all things are possible through faith, hope, and prayer. Your continued support allows us to provide uplifting resources to those in need. Whether through our communities, websites, apps, or publications, we inspire our audiences, bring them together, and comfort, uplift, entertain, and guide them. Visit us at guideposts.org to learn more.

We would love to hear from you. Write us at Guideposts, P.O. Box 5815, Harlan, Iowa 51593 or call us at (800) 932-2145. Did you love *Let It Snow*? Leave a review for this product on guideposts .org/shop. Your feedback helps others in our community find relevant products.

Find inspiration, find faith, find Guideposts.

Shop our best sellers and favorites at

guideposts.org/shop

Or scan the QR code to go directly to our Shop

Find more inspiring stories in these best-loved Guideposts fiction series!

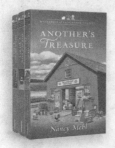

Mysteries of Lancaster County

Follow the Classen sisters as they unravel clues and uncover hidden secrets in Mysteries of Lancaster County. As you get to know these women and their friends, you'll see how God brings each of them together for a fresh start in life.

Secrets of Wayfarers Inn

Retired schoolteachers find themselves owners of an old warehouse-turned-inn that is filled with hidden passages, buried secrets, and stunning surprises that will set them on a course to puzzling mysteries from the Underground Railroad.

Tearoom Mysteries Series

Mix one stately Victorian home, a charming lakeside town in Maine, and two adventurous cousins with a passion for tea and hospitality. Add a large scoop of intriguing mystery, and sprinkle generously with faith, family, and friends, and you have the recipe for *Tearoom Mysteries*.

Ordinary Women of the Bible

Richly imagined stories—based on facts from the Bible—have all the plot twists and suspense of a great mystery, while bringing you fascinating insights on what it was like to be a woman living in the ancient world.

To learn more about these books, visit Guideposts.org/Shop